Joe Mercer
THE PICTORIAL BIOGRAPHY

Joe Mercer
THE PICTORIAL BIOGRAPHY

RICHARD BAERLEIN

Macdonald
Queen Anne Press

A Queen Anne Press BOOK

© Joe Mercer 1987

First published in Great Britain in 1987 by
Queen Anne Press, a division of
Macdonald & Co (Publishers) Ltd
3rd Floor
Greater London House
Hampstead Road,
London NW1 7QX

A BPCC plc Company

British Library Cataloguing in Publication Data

Baerlein, Richard
    Joe Mercer : the biography.
    1. Mercer, Joe   2. Jockeys——Great Britain
    ——Biography
    I. Title
    798.4'3'0924   SF336.M4/
    ISBN 0-356-12000-7

Filmset by MS Filmsetting Limited, Frome, Somerset
Printed and bound in Great Britain by Hazell, Watson & Viney Limited
Aylesbury, Bucks
A Member of the BPCC Group

PICTURE CREDITS

Agence Recoupé: 87, 88; All-Sport/Trevor Jones: Back cover, 57T, 125B, 127B; Associated Press: 49; Baron Studios: 66–7; Frank Bescoby: 112; Ed Byrne: 58–9, 120, 127T, 165, 171, 175, 184–5; Gerry Cranham: Cover, 57B, 60B, 125T, 126; Counsic Bros., Bombay: 76T, 76B; W. Everitt: 135, 136–7; Michael Haslam: 179; David Hastings: 2, 60T, 180; Alan Johnson: 181; Liberty Photos., Bombay: 74; Photo Source: 65, 84–5, 101, 108; Press Association: 24, 100, 104–5, 142, 164, Alec Russell: 12–13, 139, 141, 162, 176; George Selwyn: 147, 155, 158–9, 166, 186; Sport & General Agency: 26, 37, 42, 43, 47, 52, 69, 70, 93, 99, 114, 116–7, 132, 134, 149, 168, 172–3; Sporting Pictures (UK) Ltd: 128; Syndication International/Mirrorpic: 34; Topham Picture Library: 51

All other pictures supplied by Joe Mercer

Contents

Introduction
by Joe Mercer

It is of course a great honour to have a book written about you, and I was surprised as well as flattered when I heard that Queen Anne Press were interested in publishing my official biography.

Remembering all the good times and the magnificent horses I was lucky enough to partner made me feel almost like pulling on the old boots again, but of course I can hardly come back after finishing on such a great note at Doncaster! Being a jockey's agent these days meant that during the winter of 1986, when I wasn't shooting, I had the time to sit down and talk about the old times with Richard Baerlein and Mike Cattermole.

Richard, who is one of the senior men in the Press room, started it all off and was admirably backed up by Mike, a journalist on the *Sporting Life Weekender* and one of the younger faces to cover our sport. Mike revealed that he was my greatest fan and as our working relationship developed it became apparent that he knew more about my career than I did!

It was a fascinating task to pore over the old scrapbooks and recall a very long career. I couldn't have shared it with four better trainers than Jack Colling, Dick Hern, Henry Cecil and Peter Walwyn, and, with the sad exception of Jack, who died a few years ago, I'm delighted to be able to say that I'm still great friends with them all, and would like to thank them for all their help.

I would also like to take this opportunity to thank the editor of the book, Caroline North, and to express my gratitude to all the owners for whom I have ridden over the years and the staff who worked with me. Last, but by no means least, I would like to pay tribute to my wife Anne, who has had a lot to put up with during my career – I think she gets on better with me now than she did while I was riding!

Joe Mercer
Hermitage
May 1987

A Winner to the End

Joe Mercer will go down in the annals of the turf as the best jockey never to have won the Epsom Derby. The supreme stylist was, however, given a reception worthy of the most popular of Derby winners as he entered the unsaddling enclosure after winning the William Hill November Handicap at Doncaster on Saturday 9 November, the final day of the 1985 Flat racing season, Joe's last ride on an English racecourse.

The spontaneous applause came from the very hearts of those present. Joe had done them no favours on the 20–1 Bold Rex in beating by three lengths his stable companion Cherry Hill, a long-time ante-post favourite who drifted to 10–1 on the day. Normally such stable upsets are greeted with a stony silence and sometimes even with jeering and abuse. This was a moment to savour and Joe sat there for a few seconds before saluting the crowd as he dismounted. The warmth of the reception brought tears to Joe's eyes and even the granite-like figure of that hardened professional Alex Bird, for whom Joe had ridden many winners in days gone by, had to wipe his eyes before reaching over to offer his congratulations. Who says that racegoers speak only through their pockets? This meant more to Joe than all the written or oral tributes that followed. It was the just reward for 35 years' service to racing and to the British racegoing public.

On that momentous day the Newmarket trainer Jeremy Hindley, for whom Joe had ridden many winners in the late 1970s, was one of those who wanted to see the jockey go out with a winner. He was determined to make this a certainty by running a good two-year-old, Comme L'Etoile, who had an odds-on chance in the Armistice Stakes. Jeremy gave Joe Mercer the ride, replacing his stable jockey Michael Hills who was nevertheless promised the same present if the horse was successful. Comme L'Etoile won comfortably enough at 11–10 on. In the end, however, this perfectly executed insurance plan proved unnecessary when Joe bowed out with the big winner of the day three races later.

11

The final furlong. Joe Mercer, on his last ride, celebrates by pushing out Bold Rex to win the November Handicap.

While that was a day Joe will never forget, the 1979 season will also stand out in his memories. That season he achieved an ambition that he had been turning over in his mind even at the age of 15 – to become Champion Jockey. Thirty-two years after his first ride in public, and with over 2,500 winners under his belt since, he had grasped the Jockeys' Championship at the age of 45 from the jaws of the reigning champion, Willie Carson. At the same time he won over £1 million in win and place money for the owners whose horses he rode that year. Willie Carson had been a great rival of Joe's for many years and had even taken over his old job at Dick Hern's West Ilsley Stables in 1977. Willie never quite realised the strength of Joe's satisfaction until all the leading jockeys lined up in a team event against their American counterparts at the Bay Meadows Racecourse in California.

At the end of each season it is the custom for jockeys to disperse to such warm locations as Hong Kong, India, South Africa, Malaysia or the USA to fulfil riding engagements and enjoy a working holiday during the winter. Generally speaking, the English jockeys are very popular abroad where, because they are successful, they enjoy a very strong following. Those at the top of the tree readily find sponsors and so it was that the three leaders of the table, Joe Mercer, Willie Carson and Pat Eddery, together with Lester Piggott, were lured to California.

In the preliminaries on the track Willie Carson, as always the jester of the English party, took over the public address system to interview the English jockeys with the intention of amusing the spectators and enabling them to learn something about the riders from England. Only then did Willie learn how happy Joe was to have put one over on him at last. Willie's first question to Joe: 'What was your greatest moment in the past season?', met with a reply that completely took him aback. 'Beating you in the Jockeys' Championship.' Joe answered him with feeling.

Joe received a marvellous press throughout the later stages of that season. With three weeks to go he was quoted by Jonathan Powell in the *Sunday People* as saying: 'Now it's gone so far it would mean a hell of a lot to me to be Champion. I'd let a lot of people down if I didn't make it. So many people have said that they'd like to see me do it. I get the feeling in the weighing-room they are willing me to win.' And yet during all that time Joe still did not break his golden rule of never ringing up owners and trainers to ask for rides – he didn't need to. Joe says now that the whole of the racing world was rooting for him and indeed many trainers for whom he didn't normally ride were ringing him up to offer him mounts, and winning ones too.

Joe Mercer must be one of the very few who are not in the 'telephone jockeys' category. He says, 'It is all wrong to deprive less fortunate jockeys of their rides. One cannot admire owners and trainers who fall for this trick.' Yet when he had retired Joe had ridden well over 3,000 winners worldwide and his home record of 2,810 puts him fourth in the all-time list of leading jockeys after Sir Gordon Richards, Lester Piggott and Doug Smith. Not a bad record for a man who had never rung up for a ride!

To keep the record straight, there was just one occasion when Joe did ring up. When Billy Newnes wasn't available through injury, Henry Candy was left without a jockey for Time Charter in the 1983 King George VI and Queen Elizabeth Diamond Stakes. On hearing this news Joe's wife Anne suggested that he should 'phone Henry. Joe was reluctant but Anne persisted almost to the point of annoyance and even threatened to ring up the trainer herself if Joe didn't do it. In the end Joe relented and the rest, as they say, is history!

Jockey in the Making

The Mercer family burst into the limelight when the six-stone apprentice Manny, eldest of four sons and four daughters, won the 1947 Lincolnshire Handicap on the windswept Carholme on the 100–1 Jockey Treble. From that moment the family earned the tag of 'The Incredible Mercers' and Manny and Joe, both of whom became 'boy wonders' in the toughest of all sports, were successful way beyond the pipe dreams of their father Emmanuel and mother Jessie. Emmanuel Mercer, a coach painter in the Yorkshire woollen town of Bradford, had always wanted to be a jockey. Like so many lads of that era, he had set his mind on being a Fox, a Carslake, a Donoghue or a Gordon Richards. He was never able to accomplish his schoolboy dreams but instead was determined to inspire his sons with his own ambitions.

In Barnsley they sent their boys down the pits. In Sheffield, they went to the steel works, but in Bradford it was the mills that soaked up the young labour. Says Joe: 'I remember Lister's Mill very well. It was the biggest in England and sat on the top of a hill just out of town. Tilly, who used to run our gang, worked as one of the bobbin girls in the factory.'

The Mercer family lived in Victoria Road. There were eight children but two died very young. In order of age, they were Jessie, Manny, Doreen, Joe, Lily, Harry, Irene and Eric. All four boys were to try their hands at the racing game but Harry and Eric for various reasons failed to make it. In Harry's case, it wasn't entirely his fault. As a child he had had diphtheria amongst other problems. He went to Newmarket to begin his apprenticeship, but there the trouble began. Breathing fresh, clean air for the first time in his life had a catalytic effect on his growth. He shot up in no time and nowadays is known in the family as 'Big Harry'. 'All right, he's only five feet nine or so,' says Joe, 'but for our family, he's tall!'

Eric, meanwhile, managed to ride six winners, but grew too stocky and Joe describes him now as 'twice as wide as he is tall'. But it was Manny's success that really inspired Joe. Manny's

Through his parents and the example of his brother Manny, Joe's interest in horses was kindled at an early age.

16

career had been planned well in advance by his father. He told his friends: 'Manny will be a Champion by the time he is 21.' The difficulty lay in setting him on his path to fame because the Mercers' contacts in racing were remote. Manny's parents were keen to get him interested in horses at an early age and so Jessie Mercer went out to a local auction and, for four pounds ten shillings, bought a toy fluffy horse on wheels which became known in the family as Phoebe. Manny, as a small boy, soon got to work on Phoebe, riding imaginary races and winning by short heads. It gave the boy a feel for the game that he never lost. From there Manny graduated to donkeys at the seaside. He didn't spend his pocket money on sweets and lemonade as did most of the children of that age. Instead it went on donkey rides on the sands. He was blissfully happy and his rides on the beach were his only contact with the saddle until he went to join his first stable.

When Manny came home from school for the last time, he was told his father had written to a trainer about taking his son as an apprentice. Thousands of parents with small sons throughout the land have, over the years, written to trainers in the hope of placing their son in a stable. But only very few ever get there. While waiting for a reply, Manny went to work in Lister's Mill to build himself up. Every evening he came home and anxiously enquired if the important letter had arrived. More than eight weeks passed before the answer he was waiting for finally

Joe with his sisters Irene, Doreen and Lily at the wedding of their eldest sister, Jessie.

17

arrived. He was to start work in a racing stables. Three weeks later Jessie Mercer saw her son off at the station. His destination was Mablethorpe on the Lincolnshire coast and a stable controlled by Jim Russell. 'He weighed just over four stone and as I saw him off it nearly broke my heart,' his mother said afterwards. But she had every confidence, as she watched his tiny figure disappearing on the train, that the effort would be well worthwhile in the long run.

This was the start of Manny's brilliant but tragically short career as a jockey. He was well established as one of the best riders in the country when he was killed in a fall at Ascot on 26 September 1959. Manny had already ridden 100 winners that season but as he was going to post his mount, the filly Priddy Fair, fell and threw him against a concrete post on the rails. He sustained further head injuries as the filly struggled back to her feet.

Up to that point he had ridden the winners of the 1953 1,000 Guineas (Happy Laughter), the 1954 2,000 Guineas (Darius) as well as the inaugural running of the Washington International at Laurel in 1952 on Wilwyn. But back in the mid-1940s, Manny was just a stable lad. For three years he went through the daily stable routine and in his first year of raceriding rode only one winner, at Pontefract in his native county. But then came the great breakthrough. In 1947 he was booked by Billy Smallwood to ride a sprinter called Jockey Treble in the Lincolnshire Handicap. The trainer and the public had no confidence in his mount, which was a 100–1 chance on the day. It was only the family that was so sure that Jockey Treble would win.

At home, Jessie Mercer and Joe sat quietly listening to the radio commentary. As usual there was a large field and the starter had trouble getting them into line. Finally came the signal 'They're off' and Joe and his mother listened wordlessly as the commentator reeled off the leading horses. The field had split into two groups but there was no mention of Jockey Treble and, with two furlongs to go, their radio went flat. That was the last the Mercers heard of Manny's great triumph.

A pause followed and then Mrs Mercer turned to see a look of disappointment on Joe's face. So she finished the commentary for him: 'and the winner is Jockey Treble'. 'Has he really won?' asked the 12-year-old Joe. 'Of course he has,' said his mother – and she believed it. The next second there was a knock on the door and a neighbour burst in, shouting 'Your Manny's won! Your Manny's won!' So it really had happened as she always knew it would.

Manny's success in the Lincolnshire Handicap had shown that he was no ordinary apprentice. Shortly after this his master, Jim Russell, lost his licence and immediately George Colling, who had one of the largest stables in the country, began negotiations with Russell to transfer Manny's indentures to him. At Newmarket, Manny met Charlie Elliott, who was to play a very important part in his success story. Elliott was George Colling's first jockey and among the top three in the country. He was also strongly connected in France with Marcel Boussac, the leading owner and breeder.

Said George Colling: 'Manny picked up many tips from Charlie Elliott, but he was always a natural horseman. When Jim Russell lost his licence to train in 1947, I got on to Manny straight away. I thought he would make good. He has a wonderful pair of hands and, what is more, he is a fine rough rider – by that I mean he can sit on anything and manage the most awkward horse.'

Manny was a great inspiration for Joe in the early stages of his life. Joe says now: 'I idolised Manny in those days and used to follow his progress in the papers and in the letters he wrote home.' When Manny came home for Christmas, he faced a barrage of questions from his younger brother about horses and life in a racing stable.

When Joe was nine, his family had moved from Bradford, where he was born, to Cheadle in Cheshire. Until then, Joe's sole association with horses had been to flog the aforementioned Phoebe on whom Manny had spent so many hours. At Cheadle, Joe quickly palled up with Roy, who ran the local milk round. The milk horse knew every stop on that round and furthermore, at the end of the day, he knew his exact way back to the paddock where he was turned out. For the first time, Joe was able to sit on a real horse. It was the start of his passion for riding, from which he never looked back. He was determined to increase his involvement at every opportunity, and so on Sunday mornings he would assist the Wilmslow Riding School in mucking out and getting the horses ready twice a day for their riders. He would do anything to become associated with the animals in return for which he got the occasional ride and riding lesson. Another young lad who was a frequent visitor to Wilmslow Riding stables was Joe's school friend Gordon Reeks. (When the time came for Joe to leave home for Sparsholt and the stables of Major Sneyd, who should he meet again but Gordon Reeks, with whom he had lost touch for a year or two. Gordon was also working in the stables and he and Joe renewed their friendship.) Joe also earned

The Mercer mafia: Joe's father, Emmanuel, Uncle Fred, Manny and Joe pose proudly in front of Manny's car.

pocket money by assisting the nearby veterinary surgeon with operations, cleaning up and feeding the animals.

When he was ten, Joe and his parents went to Mablethorpe to visit Manny. There they watched the horses working on the sands and when they returned, it was simply a matter of how soon Joe could get into a racing stable. The Wilmslow Riding School had whetted his appetite but that was nothing to what he felt while he watched his brother riding work. Manny Mercer rode winners as an apprentice for Major Frederick Sneyd and Sneyd asked Manny one day if he had a younger brother. Sneyd trained at Sparsholt near Wantage and had already produced two outstanding jockeys in the Smith brothers, Eph and Doug, and when he heard about Joe he suggested to Manny that his younger brother should come for a trial during the holidays. 'So you see,' says Joe, 'I didn't choose to go to Major Sneyd, he chose me. My father went down to see him and he said that I had better come along in the summer holidays, so I went to see him when I was only 12, in 1947.'

In those days, apprentices – with the consent of their parents – practically signed their lives away to trainers from the time they first went to the stable until they reached the age of 21. Of course a successful apprentice was worth a fortune to any trainer. He could command a fee for allowing the apprentice to ride outside his stable, could insist that he was given the odds to a certain sum on any horse his apprentice rode, and get half the percentage of the stake money and expenses. In addition to this, very few trainers ever gave their apprentice at the end of his term anything like the sum that should have been stored up for the boy from the winnings during his apprenticeship. Fortunately, all this has gone by the board these days, but it is interesting that a man like Joe Mercer, who is only in his early fifties today, could have been subjected to such a rigid youth. The entire indentures, signed between the Mercer family and Major Sneyd, are reproduced here. On reading them, one can understand why Joe often repeats the old cliché that 'the modern lads do not know how well off they are!'

THIS INDENTURE WITNESSETH THAT Joe Mercer of 4 Ashfield Road, Cheadle in the County of Cheshire of the age of 12 years or thereabouts of his own free will and by and with the consent of his father who testifies his consent by executing these presents doth put himself Apprentice to Major Frederick Blair Sneyd of Eastmanton, Sparsholt, Wantage, Berks to learn his Art of a horse-trainer and jockey and with him (after the manner of an Apprentice) to serve from the 25 October 1947 unto the full end and term of the 24th October, 1955 from thence next following to be fully complete and ended. During which Term the said Apprentice his said Master faithfully shall serve, his secrets keep, his lawful commands everywhere gladly do. He shall do no damage to his said Master nor see it to be done of others, but that he shall forthwith give warning to his said Master of the same. He shall not waste the Goods of his said Master nor lend them unlawfully to any. He shall not play at Cards, Dice-tables, or any other unlawful Games whereby his said Master may have any loss with his own Goods or others during the said term without license of his said Master he shall neither buy nor sell. He shall not haunt Taverns nor Play-houses nor absent himself from his said Master's Service day or night unlawfully but in all things as a faithful Apprentice he shall behave himself towards his said Master and all his during the said term and will truly account for deliver or pay to the said Master all such moneys as the said Apprentice shall receive have or be entrusted with or which shall come to his hands or possession for or on account of the said Master or for or on account of the services of or work done by the said Apprentice during the said time and whether intended or described as presents to the said Apprentice in respect of his riding during the said term.

AND the said Major Frederick Blair Sneyd of Eastmanton, Sparsholt, Wantage, Berks hereby covenants with the said Joe Mercer that he will properly instruct and teach or cause to be instructed and taught his said Apprentice in the Art of horse-trainer and jockey which he useth by the best means that he can. Finding unto his said Apprentice sufficient Meat, Drink,

Clothing, Lodging and all other necessaries during the said term and that he shall pay to the said Apprentice three shillings a week for the first three years and ten shillings a week for the remaining term of this Apprenticeship as a gift at his option and on being satisfied as to the behaviour of the said Apprentice and will also pay him half of the riding fees as laid down by the Rules of Racing – namely half of five pounds and four shillings for a losing mount and half of seven pounds six shillings for a winning mount except the horses trained by him which he will ride free, but all presents received by the Master are hereby expressly excluded and are not to be taken into account in ascertaining such fees or otherwise.

AND for the true performance of all and every the said Covenants and Agreements either of the said Parties bindeth himself unto the other by these presents

IN WITNESS whereof the Parties above named to these Indentures interchangeably have put their hands and seals

Signed, sealed and delivered by the ⎫
above-named F. B. Sneyd   ⎬
in the presence of:—   ⎭

Joe recalls: 'Everything seemed strange at first and it came pretty hard. But it was interesting and I loved it. It didn't matter to whom you were apprenticed, you had to work very hard and they got their pound of flesh. But when you served your time in those days, you were certainly taught how to do the job properly.'

'Major Sneyd was a good guv'nor but he could be quite frightening as he growled "Look me straight in the eye, boy!" So you stood there and trembled as you looked at him with that mole on the end of his nose. It really was terrifying until you got to know him.'

Major Sneyd believed in starting his lads off at the bottom, earning their keep by doing menial tasks as weeding, gardening, stone-picking and even waiting at table. Joe says 'In those days the old man always used to dress for dinner and I used to put on a little white coat and serve him with wine and food. Later, as he got to know me better, I sat down to dinner with him and learned all the social graces.' The apprentices were entitled to only two afternoons off a week, Wednesdays and Saturdays, when they cycled into Wantage for a cup of tea and a visit to the bookmakers to see what was running. They had to be back in time for stables at 4.15 pm. They were allowed one visit to the cinema per week, but reporting back time was 11 pm. If they were late, they weren't allowed out the following week. This meant that the boys often had to come away without knowing how a film ended.

But there were ways and means of cheating the system. Joe explains: 'We all lived on the third floor in the big house. The water tanks were just outside our windows and by the side of them grew some fantastic old ivy with great, thick stems that had been there for years. We soon learned how to climb it. Come late evening, we would all say goodnight to the boss and madam. He never used to come up. In order to go out at night, we used to stash our stuff (clean shirts etc.) in the saddleroom during the daytime and then sneak down and change later. That was when the locals would lock up their daughters!

'Everything went well until I sprained my ankle at a local hop. The official story was that I had fallen out of my bunk!' The yard had a thatched roof and young Joe raised and kept ferrets which helped to keep down the rodent population, and also kept a jackdaw as a pet. He says now 'They're days I wouldn't want to go back to and do all over again. But when you look back at them, they were fun and you made your own amusement out of nothing.'

Champion Apprentice

The 'golden era' of British jockeyship is said to have been between the two wars. The majority of those performing at that time carried on after the Second World War and included Gordon Richards, Charlie Elliot, Tommy Weston and Charlie Smirke, amongst others. It was this sort of company that 15-year-old Joe Mercer joined in 1949. He recalls: 'On my first visit to the weighing-room for my first ride, on Flare Up at Brighton in 1949, I was trembling all over and felt weak at the knees. It was quite an ordeal suddenly to find oneself in the company of those men whom one regarded almost as gods. As I was led in by Major Sneyd all the valets turned away, as the Major had the reputation of being a very slow payer. Eventually, Fred Dyer, one of the valets, approached the Major and told him he was prepared to valet me on his own terms, namely that he would valet me for the entire time I was an apprentice. The Major had no alternative but to accept, because no one else was going to volunteer for the job. In the end, Fred Dyer and I became firm friends and he looked after me in the weighing-room for the next 36 years. I only had half-a-dozen rides that year but in 1950 I became a more frequent visitor to the weighing-room and formed longstanding friend-

Manny and Joe: great rivals, great friends.

ships with the other young apprentices, which included Lester Piggott, Jimmy Lindley, Derek Morris, Geoff Lewis and Edward Hide, and we tended to stick together.'

Joe's riding must have impressed because he began to attract rides from outside stables, in particular, from Bill Payne (grandfather of Newmarket trainer Pip), who had a small yard at Eastbury in Berkshire. Payne gave the 15-year-old his first winning ride on Eldoret in the two mile one furlong Portman Handicap at Bath on Wednesday, 13 September 1950. The distance of the race is a test in itself and usually finds most apprentices more tired than the horse is at the finish. Naturally, Joe was thrilled to bits, particularly as he beat Champion Jockey Gordon Richards into third place!

Four more winners came his way that year and already he had beaten Manny's record. In his first year as a jockey, Manny had ridden only one winner. For Joe there was still another to come that season, however, and what a triumph it was. Eldoret, the old handicapper, was again the horse. It was another long-distance race and as they neared the winning post it was touch and go whether Eldoret or Coup d'Epee would win. The two jockeys were hard at work and as they reached the winning post gallant old Eldoret was a neck to the good. They were led into the unsaddling enclosure and the jockey on the beaten Coup d'Epee turned to congratulate his young rival. Have you guessed it? Yes, he was Joe's idol, his elder brother Manny.

That is how they always were. Manny and Joe were the keenest of rivals on the racecourse when they were riding against each other, but they were the closest of friends off the course – not only brothers but real friends.

Just as Manny had been schooled by the great jockey Charlie Elliott, Joe found in Major Sneyd a tutor who gave him a really good grounding in riding. Sneyd proved invaluable to Joe, especially by presenting him with the rides on Capsize. 'You've heard of some horses which are described as apprentices' schoolmasters,' says Joe, 'Well, Capsize was mine and I won more races on him as an apprentice than on any other horse.' Capsize was a gelding owned by the professional backer Tom Westhead. Westhead was a very respected racegoer and a very clever one who organised numerous coups for trainers like George Todd. He was known to be a very generous man after his winners. Each time Capsize won – and he won 11 times in all – Joe collected a tenner in ready money. That was almost unheard of in those days – certainly no member of racing's hierarchy would have even considered giving a rider any 'readies' at all.

Capsize brought Joe the all-important publicity an apprentice needs when the combination brought off the Midland Autumn Double in 1952. At Birmingham, Joe had already won the Midland Cesarewitch on Misty Light, trained by Major Sneyd. The following day he rode Capsize to win the Midland Cambridgeshire. Postman's Path, ridden by Gordon Richards, was strongly fancied to win the race, but Joe beat him again on his old favourite Capsize.

A year or so later, Joe was going through the Racing Calendar when he spotted Capsize entered in a seller at Bath. Joe fancied riding him and almost at the same time the 'phone rang. It was Bill Hide, father of Edward and Tony, who had taken over Capsize, calling to offer Joe the mount. It turned out to be a happy reunion as Capsize was successful. Later, sadly, the horse met his death over hurdles.

Unlike that of his brother Manny, who shot to fame practically from the word go when Jockey Treble won the Lincoln Handicap, Joe's rise was steady but not spectacular. Nevertheless, the most important feature of those early years was the fact that Joe attracted the attention of Jack Colling, who trained at West Ilsley. Jack Colling had begun training in his native Yorkshire but later moved to Newmarket, and then to West Ilsley, where his chief patron was the Astor family. The first Lord Astor, who founded his stud before the First World War at Cliveden in Buckinghamshire, had tremendous success with his fillies, winning the Oaks five times. But he could never breed a colt capable of winning the Derby.

Colling was one of the shrewdest and cleverest members of his profession. He religiously kept a betting account down to the last detail, and in only one year did the records show he had lost. Colling was watching Mercer from the start. Joe did not ride a winner in his first year (1949) but in 1950 he rode six including the double on Eldoret. In 1951, this total went up to 15. At that time he began riding work for Jack Colling for whom Gordon Richards rode as first jockey. Joe was put up on a lot of lightweights and others when Gordon wasn't available. Now he was riding work regularly and he received a piece of fatherly advice when he met a lifelong friend in work rider Harry Grant. 'I can always remember one morning when Gordon, my brother Manny, Tommy Gosling, Frankie Barlow and myself were riding work for Mr Colling at West Ilsley,' recalls Joe. 'Harry Grant, known to all of us as "Whispering" Grant, said to me "You don't get any prizes for winning on the home gallops, you know. Gordon Richards will be riding all those that have worked well

OPPOSITE PAGE:
Joe on Capsize, on which he won 11 races as an apprentice.

27

Jack Colling, who gave Joe his first big break.

in the gallop, so if I were you I would keep a little up your sleeve and not show them up in home work."

'Well, that morning we were trying some two-year-olds. I remembered what Harry Grant had told me and thought I would not overshoot myself on my filly, Plain Justice. I could have won the gallop easily. When we got back to breakfast, the Guv'nor asked Gordon what he would be riding the following week in view of that morning's work. Gordon did not want to ride my filly so I got the ride on her.'

In a field of 39 in the Quy Maiden Stakes at Newmarket, Plain

Justice, ridden by Joe Mercer, beat the favourite Empire Stadium, ridden by Eph Smith. At the end of the 1952 season, Joe had ridden 26 winners and became Champion Apprentice for the first time.

It was Gordon Richards himself who had recommended to Jack Colling that he should take on Joe on a regular basis, although he still had two years to go before his apprenticeship with Major Sneyd was up. Joe's father had never been happy about the workings of the agreement with the Major and, like other apprentices at that time, Joe wasn't receiving the money to which he was entitled.

Joe, though still an apprentice, was given a retainer to ride as first jockey to Jack Colling in 1953. 'I had a good relationship with Jack Colling and his wife Sue. One particular morning I came in for breakfast with a plaster on my neck covering a love bite. Mrs Colling asked me what was under the plaster. "Boils, Madam," I replied. "Well, if I were you," she retorted, "I'd tell that girlfriend of yours to stop doing whatever it is she's doing to aggravate it!"' The new partnership could not have got off to a better start when Ambiguity gave the 18-year-old his first Classic winner in the 1953 Oaks at Epsom. Gordon Richards would have had the ride had he been free, but he had a contract at the time to ride for the Aga Khan, who had Kerkeb in the race.

Ambiguity, whose distinguishing feature was a big, white face, was bred by the second Lord Astor, whose father founded the famous Astor Studs before the First World War. She was by the 1942 2,000 Guineas winner Big Game out of Amber Flash by Precipitation. Big Game started a short-priced favourite for the Derby but failed because he didn't stay the trip. The late William Hill was so convinced that Big Game would not stay that he laid the colt till the cows came home. He was able, as a result, to found Hill House on his winnings and never looked back. However, on the dam's side, Ambiguity was very soundly bred, for her dam was by Precipitation, who would unquestionably have won the St Leger in 1936 had he not developed skin trouble beforehand. As a result, his stable companion, Boswell, won the race but Precipitation went on to become one of the most impressive Gold Cup winners the following year. Although Ambiguity had won the White Rose stakes at Hurst Park, which was considered quite a useful trial, she still stood at 18–1 for the Oaks. She had had only one race as a two-year-old but Joe hadn't ridden her on that occasion. He was on the winner, Persian Grove, for his old master, Major Sneyd.

Joe describes the Oaks. 'We jumped off in the middle, and

OVERLEAF:
Turning for home in the 1953 Oaks Joe's mount Ambiguity (with the big, white face) is poised to challenge. Eventual runner-up Kerkeb, with Gordon Richards up, is on the far left.

when we reached Tattenham Corner we had a nice position. I saw Gordon Richards go clear at this point and set off after him. When we reached the straight I was still behind Gordon but I knew then we were going to win.'

Ambiguity came from behind to take the lead inside the final furlong and beat Kerkeb by a length. Back in fourth place was Manny's mount Happy Laughter, who had already won a Classic for the Mercer family that season with the 1,000 Guineas. One of those watching from the stands was Jimmy Lindley, who says: 'Joe's valet Fred Dyer thought the world of him. On the day of Joe's win at Epsom, I'll never forget Fred coming up to me in the stands and saying that he thought Joe had a great chance of winning the Oaks. We watched the race together and I turned round to see tears streaming down Fred's face as Joe passed the winning post.'

Ambiguity was subsequently beaten at Newbury by a horse called Harwyn, ridden by Harry Carr ('Harry's experience beat me that day,' says Joe), but there was another big race triumph to come in the Jockey Club Cup at Newmarket over two miles and two furlongs. Overall, the riding of Ambiguity was a great performance for a young rider and Joe's mother was so proud of him that she had an oil painting depicting Joe coming in from the paddock after his Epsom victory put up in their Stockport home. That victory sealed Joe's association with Jack Colling, which lasted until Jack retired in 1962.

Ambiguity's Oaks win was the highlight of a tremendous season for Joe. He rode 61 winners and finished as Champion Apprentice for the second time. It was then that Joe decided to part company with Major Sneyd as he realised that he was not getting a square deal. He came away with about £2,000, and although that sounds a lot of money for a young lad in those days it must be remembered that the amount was supposed to include a percentage of the £15,333 earned by Ambiguity's Oaks win. There was also the retaining fee from Jack Colling to be taken into consideration.

So Joe packed his bags and went off to look for some accommodation. He found it on the lower Lambourn Road, in a little cottage right on the river Lambourn. Joe had seen an advertisement in one of the local newspapers which read, 'Accommodation for a gentleman', and thought 'Well, that's me!' so off he went. Joe takes up the story: 'This grey-haired lady opened the door. I could tell from the little bit of stout on her top lip that she'd been having a drink. I was invited in for a cup of tea and stayed there for the next five years.

'Nanny Waldron's charge for a week's accommodation was seven pounds, which sounds a lot for that time, but it included breakfast, lunch and tea and a pal allowed in for supper on Saturday night. She was a wonderful lady and a real character. I had only to drop my clothes and they were washed and ironed. She was like my mother. She used to go shopping in Newbury every Thursday as it was market day with her boyfriend, Mr Fred Lewis, who was a retired builder. I used to tease the hell out of her because every time she came back she used to have that little brown mark across her lip. She'd always deny that she'd had a drink!' Joe was allowed to bring girls home but the lounge was as far as it went. When the young jockey was courting he used to bring his girlfriends back to get Nan's opinion. But she never met Anne Carr, Joe's future wife.

After finishing riding in the North one day both Joe and Manny flew back to Cambridge together with Harry Carr, who was then the Queen's jockey. Harry invited the boys back for a drink and as they arrived at his house, the door was opened by his very pretty 19-year-old daughter, Anne. Joe describes what happened next: 'Manny, in his usual cheeky way said "Now Joe, this is the girl you should marry." Unlike the girls of today, Anne went scarlet and disappeared. She was the first girl I had ever noticed blushing and I kept thinking about her.' Ironically, Joe had originally had his eye on Anne's best friend, Joan Britt, the daughter of Edgar Britt, another jockey. 'The Tennis Club Dance

Bachelor Joe and his dog, Beauty, were well looked after by Nanny Waldron.

33

used to take place at the end of each month. They were smashing nights and used to carry on right into the early hours. I asked Joan Britt to go to the ball, but two days before, she rang to say she couldn't make it and so I ended up taking Anne.' 'It was three months before he asked me out again, though,' adds Anne.

But romance blossomed after that and it was the beginning of the end of Joe's bachelor days. Joe was delighted because all the young jocks, including Lester Piggott, thought Harry Carr's daughter was smashing. 'But she seemed to be beyond our reach,' says Joe.

OPPOSITE PAGE:
Anne Carr and Joe Mercer announce their engagement.

The Early Days

Joe Mercer's long riding career spanned two entirely different eras of raceriding. As a newcomer to the game he rode against the likes of Richards and Smirke, who were then in the autumn of their careers, and when he retired, in the same year as Lester Piggott, the racing world had found a new idol in Pat Eddery. Joe had always competed against the best but towards the end of his career it was against a different type of man and a very different style of riding.

Joe recalls the early days: 'Although I was in awe of my competitors, Major Sneyd had told me that the fastest way to improve my raceriding would be to study each one individually and to try to embrace the outstanding features of each of them. There were some very fine riders in those days and you cannot compare one generation with another. It is my opinion that the riders of that era were no better and no worse than the riders of today. Only the style has changed.'

When Joe first went into the weighing-room and was taken on by Fred Dyer, he was given a place next to Harry Carr, who was also looked after by Fred. 'Harry took me under his wing almost immediately, and with both my brother and Harry to look up to I was never short of allies. They helped me to have more confidence in myself and lose my initial reserve. It was the same when I was older – I used to get the young kids put next to me, and I would have a chat with them and get them involved.'

All apprentices coming into the racing game have their heroes and those they wish to imitate. Joe founded his style on that of his brother Manny, but regarded Michael Beary, who was by then 60 years old and someone Joe hardly knew, as the finest horseman he ever saw. Michael Beary had been the old Aga Khan's jockey for a number of years before the Second World War and had won the Oaks for him on Udaipur, among his many victories. Michael also won the 1928 Derby on Trigo for the Aga Khan's trainer, Dick Dawson, but those wins came before Joe was even born.

'In my first year, Michael Beary won the St Leger on Ridge Wood for Noel Murless, the stable jockey, Gordon Richards, having chosen the better-backed Krakatao. That was the only year I was able to assess Michael Beary, for after that he became a trainer and won the 1951 2,000 Guineas with Ki Ming. Ki Ming was owned by a Chinese restauranteur named Mr Ley On and his horse, though sprint-bred, was heavily backed for the Derby, largely because of the great confidence publicly expressed by Michael Beary. However, there were many at the time who were confident Ki Ming would not stay and it was then that they invented the immortal phrase "Lay off Ley On".

'Doug Smith, five times Champion Jockey after Gordon Richards retired, was a fine example to young riders, for he

Joe, on Nicaria, steals a march on brother Manny and Doug Smith in the Fred Darling Stakes at Newbury.

always conducted himself like a gentleman in the weighing-room. Doug was lucky in being able to ride at 7st 9lb every day of the week, rather on a par with Willie Carson who, likewise, does not have to waste. I admired the punch he pitched into his finishing efforts.

'Eph Smith was entirely different from his brother. He was a more aggressive rider and a more aggressive character, a trait for which his deafness was partly responsible. This in no way impaired his popularity in the weighing-room and I would think he was the only jockey in the world allowed to ride with a hearing aid. You could hear the thing buzzing when it was turned up full! Eph had gained his most important success when I was only five in 1939, winning the 2,000 Guineas and the Derby for Lord Rosebery on Blue Peter. I was informed that only the war prevented Blue Peter from completing the Triple Crown.

'Bill Nevett, Cock of the North for 25 years, was held in the same esteem as Gordon Richards in the South. He became one of my closest friends from an early stage. In my fourth year, when I had taken up a retainer with Jack Colling, who patronised northern meetings to a greater extent than any other southern trainer, I found myself continually back in my old county of Yorkshire. I had admired Billy Nevett, winner of three war-time

A gathering of the élite in 1959. From left: Edward Hide, Joe Mercer, Willie Snaith, Scobie Breasley, (pianist), Doug Smith, Charlie Smirke, Snowy Fordon, Stan Clayton, Edgar Britt, Harry Carr, Joe Sime, Tommy Gosling and Lester Piggott.

Derbies, from afar, when circumstances one afternoon at Pontefract initiated a longstanding friendship. I was riding a strongly fancied runner of Jack Colling's and, rounding the final bend, it seemed to me that a northern jockey, Joe Caldwell, went out of his way to impede me. After the race in the weighing-room I lost my cool. There were all the ingredients of an unpleasant situation when I made a verbal attack on Caldwell. We were about to come to blows when Billy Nevett intervened. He told us to stop the argument and said "the kid" – that was me – was right. Billy then asked me where I was staying and, when I told him I had made no arrangements, he took me back to his home, an enormous ancestral mansion.

'From that moment, I became a frequent guest at Billy's house on my visits up north. Bill had a large estate, but he was particularly proud of his four acres of gardens. His hobby was botany and he knew the Latin name of every flower in the place. When not riding he exhibited and attended every flower show, more often than not carrying off the prizes. I could not have found a better friend.

'Harry Wragg had ended a long and successful career three years before I even began. They still revered him in the weighing-room as the head waiter. As I have said, Harry Carr was the first senior jockey with whom I became associated. As the Royal Jockey, first for King George VI and then Queen Elizabeth II, Harry was respected throughout the racing world. He looked after me in the weighing-room, and if ever I was short of money he would tease Manny until he coughed up some "readies". He was a very sound and loyal stable jockey, backed up by an equally loyal Guv'nor in Captain Cecil Boyd-Rochfort. Little did I know at the time that he was to become my father-in-law!

'By the time I came along Charlie Smirke had become known to everyone as the doyen of the weighing-room. Some even went further, describing him as "The Godfather". By then he was largely concentrating on the big events, for which he was in extreme demand, especially by the old Aga Khan. The wise old Aga had realised a long time before that Smirke had no superior as a big race rider and, having won the 1936 Derby for him on Mahmoud, Smirke was still riding for him 16 years later when he won the Derby and the St Leger on Tulyar. In Smirke's last ten years he won seven Classics in all, the last being the 1958 Derby on Hard Ridden. Whatever people might say about him, he was a brilliant jockey and his record speaks for itself. Smirke defied the record books and would never admit that Gordon Richards, known then as "Moppy", was superior to him as a rider.

Champion Jockey Gordon Richards (centre) enjoys a stable lads' boxing evening with Sam Russell (back left) and trainer Herbert Blagrave (back right). The young Mercer (front right) was a keen boxer.

'Smirke was so cocky that on one occasion, when there was a good deal of uncertainty as to who would ride what for the Aga Khan in the Derby, he went about saying "Never mind what Gordon Richards rides, back me in the Derby!" Nothing gave Smirke greater pleasure than winning the race on the 100–8 Mahmoud, beating Gordon Richards on the Aga Khan's first-string Taj Akbar, which started at 6–1, three lengths. Smirke never let anyone forget that.

'Yet Gordon, as the outstanding rider of the day, was the idol of all we young apprentices, just as Lester Piggott is the modern idol. Gordon had a considerable influence on my career, because he was Jack Colling's chief rider and it was Gordon who had suggested that Colling should sign me on. There will never be another Gordon, just as there will never be another Lester Piggott. I was one of the lucky few who had the privilege of competing against both. I am often asked who was the better, but I find making such comparisons a fruitless exercise and it leads nowhere. To my intense satisfaction, there were numerous occasions when I beat them both!'

Gordon Richards' record is never likely to be beaten, in spite of the many modern improvements that have made it easier for jockeys to accumulate wins. In his day, there were often blank Mondays, there was no evening racing, and transport was nothing like as easy and quick as it is today. Yet no one since he retired has been able to ride 200 winners in a season, a feat he accomplished 12 times. In all he was Champion Jockey 26 times and his total winners, a record for this country of 4,870, represented roughly one winner in every four and a half rides. As an example of what can be done since the advent of helicopter transport, Paul Cook once rode three winners in a day at three different meetings.

Lester Piggott's supporters would claim that Gordon only won the Derby once, and that at the 27th and final attempt, whereas their hero collected nine Derbies and broke Frank Buckle's record of 27 English Classics. 'The modern generation cannot imagine that there has ever been anyone to touch Lester,' adds Joe, 'and it is a sobering thought that, while one saw Gordon striding about the racecourse as recently as 1985, no one who has come into racing over the last 32 years ever saw him ride. Nor, in those days, did we have the advantage of videos, which will provide a lasting tribute to the likes of Lester Piggott, Pat Eddery, Willie Carson and Co, so unless you examine the figures, the magnitude of Gordon's achievements can never be appreciated by those who entered racing after his retirement. At the same time, the generation which grew up with Gordon regarded him as a hero whose image was unlikely ever to be seen again. There are always likely to be three candidates for the greatest jockey of all time – Fred Archer, Gordon Richards and Lester Piggott. Modesty was the keynote of Gordon's pleasing personality.

'If you saw the style of those days compared with the style of today, you would not think it could work. We used to ride very nearly the full length of our legs and you seldom fell off, that's for sure. The reason why I started riding a lot shorter was because my ankles used to get cut to pieces. We had those big, long lead cloths with a stack of lead in front – you would be chafing your ankles all the time. Then the rubber girth came in, with rather bulky leathers on the side, so that as your legs passed the saddle flap, it wasn't smooth when you kicked on. I used to cut my ankles to shreds and get through a pair of boots in ten days.

'Only two firms made racing breeches in those days, Goldings and Chesters, both in Newmarket. For the sake of smartness, and believe me they were smart, they had little pearl buttons starting just below the knee, which went halfway down your leg. These tended to turn inwards as you rode and then you had the imprint

41

Joe (number 30) beats his father-in-law, Harry Carr, into third place. Note the length of the riders' irons.

on your shin-bone and this proved very painful. I have marks which will be with me for the rest of my life, on my ankles and shin-bones, due to the tack in vogue at the time. The Australians were way ahead of us in every department of racing tack. It was through them, and through the English jockeys riding in India, that the gradual change in fashion was brought about.

'Lester was the pace-setter in all this, because he began riding abroad at a very early age. He was continually bringing back improvements in saddlery and tack which he had seen in other countries, especially Australia, and I give Lester, along with the influx of Australian riders, the credit for bringing us up to date. For instance, Lester was the first ever to use goggles, which he had discovered in America. They made a tremendous difference to our riding, especially when the ground was firm and the dust was flying. Before the days of goggles, you would come back with your eyes sore and the dust making it hard to see where you were

Joe wins a handicap at the now defunct Lewes track. By now most riders were wearing goggles.

going during the race. The whole scene changed almost overnight. Curiously enough, the firm in England which manufactured goggles used to send their entire output to the United States and then, after Lester's visit, some would filter back here. Other items trickled in with the influx of the Australian jockeys. Scobie Breasley, for example, used to bring back smart saddles from Australia that were of a far better design than ours.

'As a result of his frequent visits abroad, Lester also began to change his riding style. Especially noticeable was the shortening of his stirrup level. Automatically this trend became the fashion and, with the better equipment, it seemed to work. Lester is a law unto himself, his balance is simply unbelievable. Anyone who tries to copy him is just an idiot.

'Almost entirely due to Lester, English jockeys today ride shorter than their Australian counterparts, whereas, before Lester adopted his new style, it was the Australians who rode the shorter. The contrast in style over the 35 years of my riding career, between the heyday of Gordon and the heyday of Lester, is probably no less marked than the difference between the days of Fred Archer and Gordon Richards. There is no doubt, though, that the style and equipment of today gives raceriding a far neater and more professional appearance.'

There is no doubt either that riding these days is more comfortable than it was when Joe started. He goes on: 'When I began you had a brown pair of breeches for wet days and they were supposed to be waterproof. Well, that was a joke – I used to come back absolutely wet through which meant I had to change after every race. Now, there are some super waterproof breeches as well as waterproof boots with rubber soles.

'There's nothing worse than waiting behind the stalls when it's peeing down and the water's running down your back and everything gets wet, jockstrap and all! But you forget all about it as soon as the race starts. In the spring and autumn of my early days, the first thing I used to do was catch a cold. So I had one for the first month of racing and also for the last because I was always soaked through!'

West Ilsley – Jack Colling

In 1954 Joe Mercer and Lester Piggott were joint Champion Apprentices, Lester having won the title in 1950 and 1951. But Joe was now also a Classic-winning jockey. Amazingly, Ambiguity was to be his only Epsom Classic win. Lester of course was to win the 1954 Derby on Never Say Die, the first of his 14 Classic victories at Epsom, of which a record nine were in the Derby.

Joe was now firmly established as first jockey to Jack Colling but he was also getting some interesting outside rides. One of them was a particularly fortuitous one. As a result of Scobie Breasley suffering a bad injury in a fall at Alexandra Park in late May, trainer Noel Cannon used Joe for quite a number of his horses that year. Thus Joe ended up with the ride on the 1,000 Guineas winner Festoon in the Oaks. Festoon, who ran in the colours of John Dewar, famous for Tudor Minstrel, had already made all the running under Scobie Breasley in the Newmarket Classic and Joe must have been hopeful of following up his win on Ambiguity at Epsom. But it was not to be. Festoon didn't quite stay but proved herself an outstanding miler when she won the Coronation Stakes at Royal Ascot by a comfortable four lengths. This was Joe's first winner at the Royal Meeting and he completed a double with Summer Solstice for trainer Derrick Candy in the Windsor Castle Stakes.

Around this time, Joe struck up a friendship in the weighing-room with Jimmy Lindley and the two are still great mates today. Says Jimmy: 'My boss Towser Gosden and one of his owners, Alex Bird, were great fans of Joe's and, as I was always about 7lb heavier than Joe, he often came in for the rides at around the eight-stone mark. He rode many a good winner for them, such as Precious Heather, V-Sign and Orthopaedic.'

There is a story to tell about Precious Heather. The colt had won the 1956 Ayr Gold Cup under Edward Hide and Alex Bird was convinced that Precious Heather would win the Lincoln Handicap if he could be held up to get the trip. In late November 1956, Bird arranged a gallop at Lingfield just over a week after

45

the Flat season had ended. There were five horses taking part and Joe held up Precious Heather, who according to the jockey, 'worked exceptionally well'. In his autobiography *The Life and Secrets of a Professional Punter*, Bird recalls: 'After the gallop, Towser and I took the jockeys for lunch at a nearby hotel. Over a brandy, I pulled Joe aside and told him that Precious Heather would win the Lincoln if ridden with the patience he showed that day. "But keep it quiet and there will be a very good present for you." I said.'

Within days of the market opening for the Lincoln the following spring, however, the price for Precious Heather had tumbled dramatically. But not a penny of it was Bird's money. There had been a leak somewhere and Alex didn't even get a chance to take what he describes as 'the pickings of the market'. It could mean only one thing. Alex Bird arranged to meet Joe Mercer in the Compleat Angler at Marlow.

Apparently what had happened was that Joe, spending one of his early holidays abroad in Monte Carlo, had gone along to watch at a casino and had told a losing gambler that he could get some of his money back on Precious Heather in the Lincoln. Unfortunately, though he didn't know it, Joe had made a major blunder, for the man was none other than bookmaker Chummy Gaventa. Bird's reaction was to take Precious Heather out of the Lincoln despite the pleas of the trainer. Joe completes the story: 'I finally rode Precious Heather in the Lincoln the following year and though he ran well to get placed he didn't get the trip. So it is possible he may not have won in 1957 either, particularly as the 1958 race was won by Babur, who had won the race the previous year.'

Joe has always said that the best horse he ever rode during his association with Jack Colling was Hornbeam, who raced from 1955 to 1958. Hornbeam won 11 races from a mile to two miles worth £10,635, which by today's standards wouldn't amount to first prize in a fair handicap. Hornbeam, who was also second nine times, is described by Joe as 'a really good horse on his day and probably unlucky not to have won a Classic. He was always getting beaten necks and half lengths in races like the St Leger, the Ebor and the Gold Cup.' Jack Colling in fact had a good record with stayers, winning plenty of races with them during this time including Rally (1956 and 1957 Brown Jack Stakes, 1958 Queen Alexandra Stakes), Nick La Rocca (1953 Northumberland Plate and dead heat with Souepi in the Doncaster Cup in the same year) and Master of Arts (1958 Northumberland Plate).

Hornbeam was a chestnut son of Hyperion, and according to

his jockey 'had a wonderful, placid temperament'. He won four of his eight starts as a three-year-old, including the Great Voltigeur Stakes at York, and finished in the frame in the Derby (fourth to Lavandin) and St Leger (runner up to Cambremer). According to Joe, 'Hornbeam stayed very well and had to have a strong gallop so we often had to force the pace. Nowadays a horse like Hornbeam would probably have a pacemaker. But then it was different. When you get a horse like that, that can get down to his work and just slog it out, then you have a great horse.

Joe goes to post on Hornbeam. For many years he considered him the best horse he had ridden.

47

'We were beaten a short head for the Doncaster Cup and a head in the Yorkshire Cup. When he was beaten half a length in the Ebor he was trying to give the winner Morecambe 23lb. The following year Morecambe won the Cesarewitch with 9st 1lb.'

One of Hornbeam's victories came in the Winston Churchill Stakes at Hurst Park. On that day, a beautiful Whitsummer Saturday, the Queen managed to escape from her duties to see her colt Atlas, who was strongly backed to win that race. Joe got a lot of credit for riding a particularly brainy race on Hornbeam, for he suddenly slipped his field just before the bend in the straight, turning for home with a six-length advantage. From that point, he was just able to hold on by a short head from the French challenger, Clichy. The Queen's colt Atlas was just threequarters of a length behind in third place.

The previous year, on 23 May 1955, English jockeys had been confronted with an entirely new phenomenon – evening racing. The first-ever London meeting took place at Alexandra Park and there was such an enormous crowd that it took over half an hour to drive the last two miles from Islington. The crowds were still pouring in as the first race was being run. Evening racing was to give jockeys far more opportunities as they could now ride at two meetings on the same day. That is why 23 May 1955 is a day Joe Mercer will never forget. He had ridden five races in the afternoon at Leicester and was placed in every one. He then came down to Alexandra Park. He did not have a ride in the first race, which was won by his friend Jimmy Lindley on Alex Bird's Tobasco, which was backed from 5–1 to 7–4. However, Joe won on his first mount at the meeting, Miss Honey. Joe's father-in-law, Harry Carr, also had a winner and Doug Smith completed a double. Joe had two further rides in which he was placed, and so he ended the day with the remarkable record of having been placed in eight races.

Joe did even better at Windsor on 27 June 1956 when Shining Grass, Tobasco, Grey Magic and Clyde Light combined to produce his first four-timer.

During the late 1950s, Joe struck up a fine partnership with a filly called Rosalba, undoubtedly one of the best that Jack Colling ever trained. Joe described her as, 'brilliant over six furlongs to a mile'. Rosalba, who was by the 1945 2,000 Guineas winner Court Martial, won the Convivial Stakes at York and the Cornwallis Stakes at Ascot as a two-year-old in 1958. As a three-year-old she won the Fred Darling Stakes at Newbury on her reappearance and then met her only defeat over a mile when running second to the great Petite Etoile in the 1,000 Guineas.

With Petite Etoile taking on the middle-distance performers afterwards, Rosalba mopped up in the Coronation Stakes at Royal Ascot and the Queen Elizabeth II Stakes on the same course. She wasn't quite so good at sprint distances but still had the speed to run third in the July Cup.

The Epsom Derby meeting of that year was to prove an eventful one for Joe – in more ways than one. Owners have always been very fickle and hard to please when it comes to engaging jockeys. Some trainers make no bones about it and regard owners as a necessary evil. Whatever they feel, that opinion is being put further and further into the background these days as the struggle to fill the vacant boxes in stables becomes the number one priority.

Trainer Harry Wragg at Abingdon Place with work riders Manny, Peter Robinson and Joe.

49

There have been occasions when a trainer has felt strong enough to tell an owner who did not want the stable jockey to ride for him in a particular race to take his horses elsewhere, but that has become a rarity. Others express disapproval but accept the situation to avoid aggravation, especially if the stable jockey is to receive the same present as the man who takes his place. But for a top jockey to be replaced by Lester Piggott, as was the case when Joe Mercer was due to ride Nagami in the 1959 Coronation Cup, was a move that was frowned upon from all sides. By that time Joe had become a top flight rider and it was six years since he had ridden his first Classic winner. He was in demand to ride for such selective trainers as Paddy Prendergast and Harry Wragg, apart from his long-running retainer with Jack Colling.

To put as polite a slant on the case as possible, an owner's superstition was said to have prevented Joe Mercer from riding Nagami, winner of the Coronation Cup. The horse, owned by Mrs Etti Plesch, wife of the Hungarian merchant banker, Apard Plesch, was ridden by Lester Piggott. But Joe had turned up at the course expecting to ride Nagami. Said Mrs Plesch 'I am a superstitious woman and I felt that I must give Lester the mount, as he won on Nagami in Milan last Autumn.' Joe responded: 'I was not told until I got to the course that I was not riding Nagami. After this I don't want to ride Nagami or any other horses owned by Mrs Plesch again.' Mrs Plesch said that she thought Joe was a 'great jockey' and then added, 'I shall treat him just as if he had won the race himself.' The prize was then £3,265.

The last-minute switch of jockeys also upset Nagami's trainer, Harry Wragg, who said, 'I told Mrs Plesch that she couldn't do this to a top class jockey like Joe. I was very upset about it.' At the time, it appeared that the rift between Joe Mercer and Mrs Plesch would mean finding another jockey to ride Nagami in the King George VI and Queen Elizabeth Stakes at Ascot the next month. Instead, Nagami was switched to the Grand Prix de St Cloud, a course over which he had won earlier in the year. However, he finished only eighth of ten to Herbager. On his final run in the Ebor Handicap, Nagami was ridden by Manny Mercer to finish fifth to Primera. So Joe lost nothing by refusing to ride Nagami again.

Earlier that year Joe had tied the knot with Anne Carr, daughter of Royal jockey Harry. Poor Anne must have had her loyalties torn as she watched the Derby that year. Her father describes the closing stages of the race in his book *Queen's Jockey*.

OPPOSITE PAGE:
Joe and Anne on their big day at St Paul's Church, Knightsbridge.

'I had Parthia where I wanted him as we turned into the straight, and in the last furlong I passed my son-in-law Joe Mercer on Harry Wragg's Fidalgo and, with somewhat mixed feelings, stopped him from riding his first Derby winner. We were first and second, with the French-trained Shantung third.'

Harry Carr finishes the account of the race: 'Joe, however, was in his twenties, and I in my forties, and as we came in I said that he had plenty of time yet while I was not far off being an old-stager.'

You would probably have been led away by men in white coats if you had suggested then that that was as close as Joe Mercer was going to get to winning the Derby. But that was how it turned out; he was beaten a longer distance on Relkino when second to Empery in 1976. Fidalgo, incidentally, provided Joe with some consolation in the Irish Sweeps Derby at the Curragh and later ran second to Cantelo in the Leger. But, as we know, 1959 was to end tragically for the Mercer family with the death of Manny at Ascot in late September.

On a much happier note, Joe was now established as a top flight jockey, and was earning enough to treat himself to a few of the luxuries in life – like a sports car. 'We used to do a lot of motoring in those days' says Jimmy Lindley. 'Joe loved cars. He had a big XK 140 and I had an Austin Healey. We were going across the Pennines to Manchester one day and we were really travelling when we saw a car in front of us. Joe whipped past it as a lorry was coming towards us which caused this car to almost climb the bank to miss Joe as he cut in in front. I had to overtake as well, of course, and as I was passing I looked across to see this recognisable face glaring at me. "I think we've done it this time," I said as we both got out at the Grand Hotel in Manchester. "Why's that?" "Well the fellow we blew off the road was Alec Marsh, the Chief Starter!"'

Jimmy and Joe, along with Derek Morris, were known in the weighing-room as 'the three musketeers'. They had many holidays together. Jimmy Lindley again: 'I think the first holiday that we paid for out of our own pockets was in Mallorca. Derek Morris had just married Myra and there was Joe and Anne, my wife Pat and myself. One evening we were watching this big Spanish girl doing a cabaret. Joe got hold of her in the dressing-room and for a bit of a laugh asked her to chat up Derek in front of his new wife. She obliged, and towards the end of the evening she had Derek up on the stage and was giving him a peck or two. After about the fourth night of this, poor Myra had just about had enough. Joe, who had heard that the cabaret was moving on

OPPOSITE PAGE:
Coming second to Parthia in 1959 on Fidalgo was the closest Joe Mercer came to winning the Epsom Derby. However, compensation was to come at the Curragh.

53

Joe's pride and joy.

*The Three Musketeers.
Unfortunately this skiing
holiday in Gstaad came to
an abrupt end when funds
ran out!*

down the road, said: "I quite agree, Myra. This has got to stop. We won't use this club again, we'll go to the one down the road."

'Myra was a lot happier until the curtain went up for the cabaret. Joe was under the table in hysterics while Derek and Myra were arguing about whether their marriage would last as long as the holiday!'

Jimmy Lindley recounts another amusing story, this time from Barbados. 'Anne, Joe, Pat and I spent a winter holiday there. John Sutcliffe also came out and at the time was going out with Caroline Tennant – a cracking girl and a lot of fun. Anyway, as we were coming back one night from the The Bearded Fig Tree, Joe said to me: "Go on Jimmy, lend Caroline your sweater as it's getting a bit chilly." The sweater I had on was cashmere and I'd saved all season for one. Gallantly, I put it around the girl's shoulders, only to see her promptly walk into the sea and have a swim in it! There were roars of laughter coming from Joe ... until I told him that it was his identical sweater that I had borrowed from him!'

Derek Morris and Joe 'The Coat' window-shop in Geneva. Jimmy Lindley isn't tempted.

West Ilsley – Dick Hern

At the end of the 1962 season Jack Colling announced his retirement as trainer at West Ilsley. He had trained there for the Astor family since 1949. His last season was rather an anticlimax in that the colt Escort, of which big things had been expected, turned out to be quite a rogue, although he did finish fourth to Larkspur in the Derby. That was the year seven horses fell as they were going downhill into Tattenham Corner. One of them, Hethersett, had started favourite for the race and judging by the way he defeated Larkspur in the St Leger he would probably have won at Epsom.

Hethersett was owned by Major Lionel Brook Holliday and his private trainer was another Major, Dick Hern. Hern, who was Champion Trainer for the first time in 1962, took over from Jack Colling at West Ilsley. Joe Mercer, of course, remained as stable jockey. Joe reflects: 'Fortunately for me Jakie Astor chose Dick to take over. I'd known him for years and had ridden for him when he was training for Major Holliday at Newmarket and also when he was assistant trainer to Michael Pope. So we really understood each other and got on really well from the start.'

Among the horses left by Jack Colling was the five-year-old Darling Boy, who had already proved himself a top class handicapper. At five, like many horses, he was to prove better than ever and Dick Hern must have had slightly mixed feelings when he saddled Darling Boy for the Jockey Club Stakes at Newmarket in April 1963, for the odds-on favourite was none other than Hethersett, who was now trained by Jack Meaney. Darling Boy, who had had the advantage of a previous run, handed out a decisive beating to Hethersett, who was ridden by Harry Carr. Hethercett ran only twice more after that, putting in by far his best effort on the first occasion when he came off very much second best against the brilliant Exbury in the Coronation Cup. Darling Boy though, added another valuable prize to his tally in the form of La Coupe de Longchamp in May over a mile and threequarters. It was Joe's first winner in France and Dick

OPPOSITE PAGE. ABOVE:
So much for the diet! Joe demolishes a packet of sweets between races.

BELOW:
Royal Ascot 1980. Le Moss maintains his advantage over Ardross in a vintage Gold Cup.

With Kris, who won 14 of his 16 starts at the highest level between 1978 and 1980. Here, in the penultimate race of his career, Kris is in full gallop as he strides clear at Goodwood.

Joe's last Royal Ascot winner – 31 years after his first! Marouble, trained by Charlie Nelson, in the unsaddling enclosure following his success in the Norfolk Stakes.

The immortal Brigadier Gerard, arguably the best English-trained horse since the War, makes it 15 out of 15.

and Sheilah Hern and Joe's wife, Anne, were all there to see it. Darling Boy then finished a creditable fourth to Ragusa in the King George VI and Queen Elizabeth Stakes at Ascot.

The Hern–Mercer combination carried on the stable's tradition of doing particularly well in the staying races. That was no surprise, for their patrons specialised in breeding stayers. One of them was Lord Astor's chestnut son of Alycidon called Grey of Falloden, who was to become a firm favourite with the public in the 1960s. The peak of Grey of Falloden's long and distinguished career was probably when, as a five-year-old, he humped a record 9–6 to victory in the 1964 Cesarewitch Handicap. 'He was a tremendous handicapper and a wonderful horse to ride' is how Joe summed him up. As a six-year-old Grey of Falloden was not surprisingly handicapped to the hilt, although he ran some fine races in defeat when placed in the Northumberland Plate and the Queen's Prize. But he managed to gain two more wins in conditions races. In the Henry II Stakes at Sandown Joe's super tough mount gave 7lb and a beating to Fighting Charlie who went on to win the Ascot Gold Cup. As a gelding, Grey of Falloden was not permitted to run in the Gold Cup (indeed it was only in 1986 that this absurd rule was relaxed and geldings were allowed to run for the first time) and instead he registered a comfortable win in the Queen Alexandra Stakes.

Racehorses of 1965 pays a fitting tribute to this old favourite: 'Grey of Falloden prospers on hard work, and though he wears blinkers, it is not because of any fault in his courage. Indeed, he is as game a horse as one would wish to find.'

In fact 1965 was a particularly good year for the Astor family. As well as Grey of Falloden, the Viscount had Craighouse while his brother, Jakie, had Provoke. It was Provoke, a son of Aureole, that was to give Joe his second record domestic Classic winner after a 12-year gap. Joe recalls: 'Provoke was a little difficult as a two-year-old and it was October before we could do anything with him. In those days we took a lot of backward two-year-olds to Newbury races to give them a bit of experience. We'd line them up at the turn and work them the other way round. Provoke went on two or three occasions and started putting it together. I said to the lad that did him that this could be a really nice horse one day. Dick Hern said that from the moment I said that, the lad changed his attitude to the horse, the horse changed his, and everything went the right way.'

After Provoke had gained his third win in succession in the Melrose Handicap at York, it was decided to run him in the St Leger – to try to get third place! Meadow Court, runner-up to Sea-

Soaked racegoers watch in disbelief as Provoke leaves the odds-on Meadow Court standing in the 1965 St Leger.

Bird in the Derby, was considered by most to be the ready-made winner. Joe reflects on the events that led up to the race: 'It poured with rain for three solid days before the St Leger. The more it rained the more Provoke would like the ground. Well, the rain was so heavy it was unbelievable. Come the day of the race, it peed down all day and the more it rained the more we thought "we've got a chance here". With all the rain visibility was poor, and when the spectators saw this mud-splattered horse emerging from the haze they all thought it was Meadow Court. But it was me!' Provoke the 28–1 outsider had beaten the 11–4-on favourite, Meadow Court, by a staggering ten lengths. 'Coming back to the unsaddling enclosure, somebody must have whacked him on the backside because he bucked and sent me shooting up in the air.'

Craighouse completed the double for Joe that year by winning the Irish St Leger at the Curragh in only his fourth race. He had been introduced that year in the Wood Ditton Stakes when he had made hacks of the opposition. With both Provoke and Craighouse the stable looked set to mop up in the Cup races in 1966 but it was then that the stable was first hit by a series of viral infections that endured on and off for three seasons. In the book *Eight Flat Racing Stables*, Dick Hern told John Rickman: 'We had an absolutely terrible time. The 'flu had completely crucified my string. It was so bad that we even took the tan out of the covered ride and replaced it with sand. That was how desperate we had become. It was nearly driving me mad but I realised there was little to be done except sweat it out . . .'

62

Both Provoke, who never ran again after the Leger, and Craighouse were finished by the virus and were subsequently shipped off to Russia as stallions. Unfortunately, Provoke died very soon after getting only one mare in foal. Joe remembers: 'We were having a very good spell too up until the virus. We seemed to shake it off in 1967 but then it struck again.' By this time though, Joe had built up a large clientele in the Berkshire district and was riding the first choice of horses for Derrick Candy, Peter Walwyn, Jeremy Tree and others. Whenever Paddy Prendergast sent over a two-year-old for Chester or York, he too was only too pleased to employ the services of Joe Mercer.

'I rode for Derrick Candy on and off for donkey's years and during that time I only had one disagreement with him, and that led to him not putting me up for about six months. It concerned a so-called "gentlemen's agreement" of ours, that I rode for him whenever available. In those days Les Hall was one of the best gambling trainers and I rode a moderate horse of his at Brighton which got beaten when it should have won. I told Les he'd given me the wrong instructions and agreed to ride the horse in a seller at Sandown the following week. Two days before the race Derrick rang up and asked if I was riding his in the same race and I said I was already booked and that we should have sorted it out a week before. He said "Right, thank you very much" and slammed the 'phone down! It wasn't until the following year that he asked me to go and ride work again and during that time he'd had a hell of a spell: at least Les Hall's trotted up in the seller!'

But in 1967 the Candy–Mercer partnership was running smoothly and it was that year that Parbury gave them both their first win in the Ascot Gold Cup. Joe rode a peach of a race to beat Doug Smith on the line on Mehari. Another notable success was the win of Fair Winter in Goodwood's Nassau Stakes. The filly was owned by William Barnett and later produced one of the family's best horses in Master Willie.

By August of that year Joe was having such a tremendous season that he was clear at the top of the Jockeys' Championship. Thirty-two-year-old Joe must have had high hopes of staying there, such was the form of the Hern horses at the time. But then disaster struck. While riding at Folkestone on 17 August Joe's mount, Native Copper, broke a leg and in the ensuing fall Joe seriously fractured his spine between the shoulders. 'Mercer Hurt: Title Bid is Dashed' the headlines read. Joe describes the preceding events: 'I had been in Sweden and was late coming back on the Monday when I had several mounts at Folkestone. I had fixed up an aircraft but when I got to the airport, Steve

Stanford, who has been marvellous to the jockeys over the years, said that the weather was too bad to fly. He told me that there was a train that left from London and so I immediately drove there to catch it.

'After I had boarded I was told by the guard that the train didn't stop at Weston Hangar: "But I know who you are," he said, "We'll slow it down!" Sure enough, it got slower and slower and I jumped off and ran like hell to the races. My first intended mount had already won but I won the fifth race on Drinka Pinta, my 78th winner of the season. I wasn't going to stay for the last but Duncan Keith, who was having problems with his weight, told me that Bill Wightman's runner, which he was down to ride, would win. I thought to myself, "Well, if he thinks it will win, I'll ride it."

'At Folkestone there are dips here, there and everywhere and I was leading the field with just over two furlongs to run when coming out of one of these dips. It was then that the horse broke its leg and that was the last I remember. It was the end of me for the season!'

Joe was taken to Ashford General Hospital before being moved to the London Clinic the following day. He was sedated during the move. A side-effect of sedatives is that they make people talk and apparently Joe's mother-in-law, who was present, was given a real eye-opener as to what her son-in-law was really like! The X-rays had revealed two crushed vertebrae but doctors were quick to point out that he would not suffer any permanent disability. At the time of the accident Joe was seven ahead of his nearest rival, Scobie Breasley. 'Without doubt, I would have won that year,' says Joe now. He spent ten days in the Clinic and Scobie, Jimmy and the lads all paid a visit. The nurses couldn't even use their own refrigerators so full were they of champagne and caviar brought for Joe. He was told to do nothing for three months. So Joe decided, after being discharged from hospital complete with surgical collar, to go off on his own for a while and he visited Scandinavia before ending up in Spain. 'I didn't do a thing,' he says, 'and I got rather fat from all the eating and drinking.'

Finally Joe was given the go-ahead to resume riding and he decided in January 1968 to go to India, where the lovely warm climate was perfect for restoring peak fitness. Joe had first been to India in 1960 and had been back several times since after enjoying a lot of success. It was there that he sat on a horse for the first time since his accident: 'I only went for a trot but my legs had gone and I couldn't see anything but stars. It took me about a

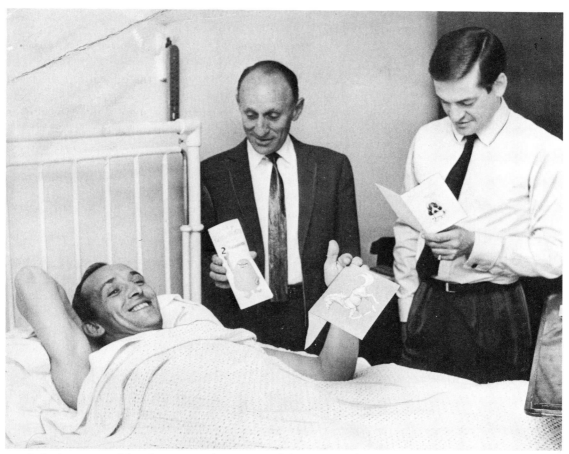

week before I could ride out without a problem. But after a while, the fat just fell off and everything was going fine.' That was, until Joe decided to play a practical joke.

Anne had joined him in India and as she was lying down one day taking the sun, Joe couldn't resist the old trick of pouring some cold water on her. Anne's reaction accidentally smashed the glass Joe was holding which badly cut Joe's hand. The bleeding had to be stopped before it could be operated on and Joe lost a lot of blood. He regained consciousness to see Geoff Lewis's face looking down at him. A big gamble that had been planned had been landed in Joe's absence and the first thing that Joe heard was that the medical bills would all be paid for by the successful connections.

Poor Joe had his arm in plaster for seven weeks and the only advantage was that he found he could play snooker better with it on. Somehow or other the cue would rest perfectly. Little wonder Joe reflects that 1967 was 'a strange year'.

Well-wishers Scobie Breasley and Jimmy Lindley find Joe in good spirits after his Folkestone accident.

OVERLEAF:
West Ilsley stables. Joe and Tree Leopard with Henry Mercer in the saddle.

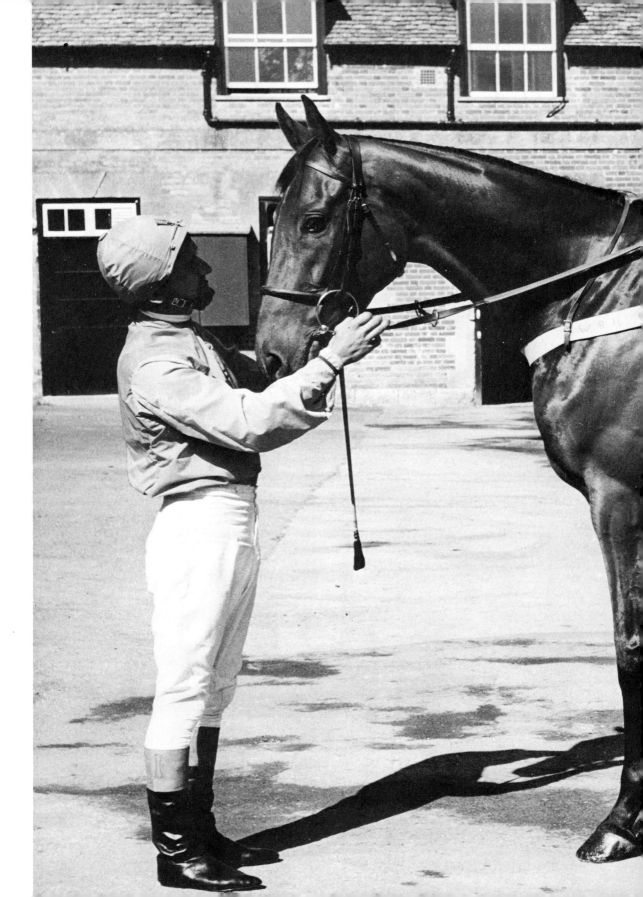

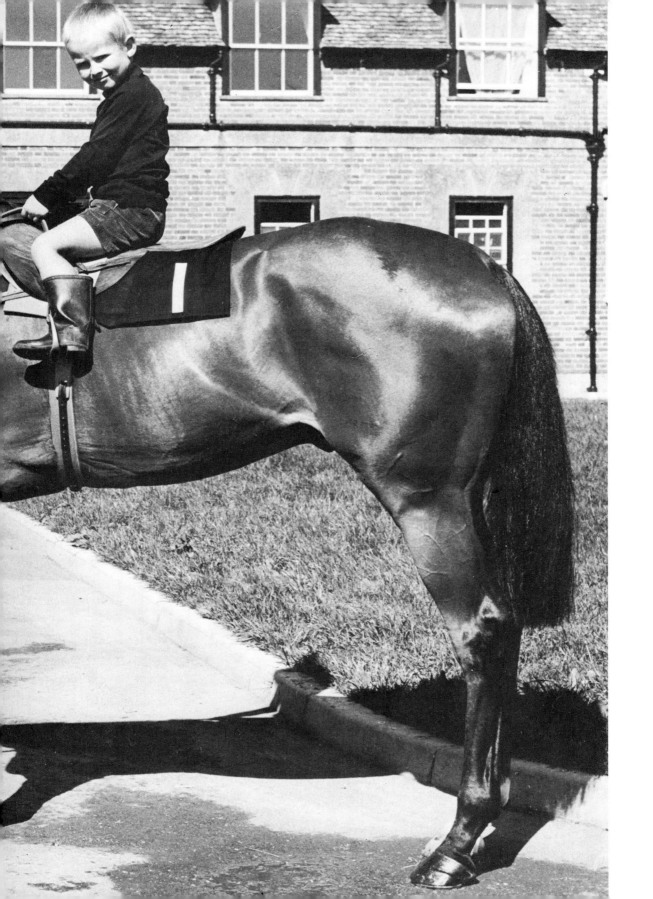

Before the accident, Joe had partnered a chestnut colt called Remand to win the Bulford Maiden Plate at Salisbury on his racecourse debut. Joe's injury prevented him from partnering Remand in his two remaining races and Lester Piggott, who eventually took the Jockeys' Championship with 117 winners, deputised in the Solario Stakes at Sandown and the Royal Lodge Stakes at Ascot. Remand, a son of Alcide, won these races too in good style and went into winter quarters well fancied for the Derby.

West Ilsley made a good start in 1968 – everything was going well right up to and including the Chester May Meeting. In his Derby trial Remand put up a workmanlike display to beat Connaught, who received 4lb, by half a length in the Chester Vase. Remand was to start second favourite for the Derby having won all four of his starts. The favourite off-course was Sir Ivor, who had already won the 2,000 Guineas in brilliant fashion. Joe remembers the Guineas well: 'Early in the spring, Sam Armstrong approached me to ride Petingo in his Guineas trial as well as in the big race itself as Lester, who had ridden Petingo as a two-year-old, had chosen to stick to Sir Ivor. Petingo won the Craven Stakes very easily but although he ran a super race in the Guineas, he was beaten by a better horse in Sir Ivor. Lester was grinning all over his face after the race and was in his best mocking mood: "I was always behind you" he chortled. But I felt that I would get my revenge at Epsom.' In the 1968 Derby, Lester was afraid of only one horse – Remand!

After Chester, however, the Dick Hern stable began to have problems with sickness again. As Joe says, 'It got so bad that we had to shut up shop for a few weeks a bit later on. Towards the back-end we had a filly who should have run in the Oaks trying to win a maiden at Folkestone. It was really sad. The horses just picked grass all day and wouldn't even jump or kick. The vets couldn't pinpoint the problem but I remember that the horses' eyes weren't right – they were very bloodshot. It took a long, long time to clear up and it got to the stage where anything that barked in the yard was cleared out.' Joe laughs now, adding: 'I remember Dick's old hack coughing and him threatening to "shoot the bastard!"'

Unfortunately Remand, like all the rest, fell foul of the virus and was a sick horse when he ran in the Derby. Joe reflects: 'You wouldn't have recognised the horse in the paddock at Epsom from the week before. He had just fallen apart and was a shadow of the Remand I knew.' In the circumstances Remand ran an excellent race to finish fourth, beaten five lengths by Sir Ivor.

Connaught, who had been beaten by Remand at Chester, was second, beaten a length and a half. 'It's hard to say, but I think he would have won if he'd been well. He was a very, very good horse.' Remand didn't run again as a three-year-old and although he came back to win the Westbury Stakes and the Cumberland Lodge Stakes as a four-year-old he was never quite the same horse again.

At least there were some excellent outside rides in 1968. That year, Derrick Candy had a very fast two-year-old son of Sing-Sing, named Song. Joe partnered the colt in its most important success that year in the New Stakes at Royal Ascot. Now called the Norfolk Stakes, the race was won in 1986 by Song's son Sizzling Melody. Joe then achieved the Royal Ascot sprint double with Jeremy Tree's d'Urbeville. Jimmy Lindley had ridden a lot of Dick Hern's horses in 1967 after Joe's injury but this time it was Joe who picked up a spare ride from Jimmy, who was unable to do the weight at 8st 3lb. In those days the three-year-olds used to receive all the advantages from their elders and the King's Stand was very much the 'Getting Out' Stakes. But although d'Urbeville was very fast, he was not rated as good a

The muscular frame of Song is at full stretch as Joe drives him home to beat Bill Williamson on Lord John in the 1968 New Stakes at Royal Ascot.

winner of the King's Stand Stakes as Song, who won the race the following year in 1969. 'Song was a very good horse and one with terrific acceleration. I would think he was the fastest horse I have ever sat on. He was built like a tank and really looked the part. He was best when tucked in behind, and once pulled out, he used to fly.' In 1969 Song won the Abernant, Temple, King's Stand and Diadem Stakes to establish himself as champion sprinter in a vintage year that included Tower Walk, Be Friendly and So Blessed. Song had lost the Nunthorpe Stakes at York after putting up a temperamental display beforehand and he was retired after his only race as a four-year-old as a result of repeating that behaviour. Fortunately it didn't affect his stud career, which has been very successful and includes three winners of the Flying Childers Stakes.

Derrick Candy was just as adept at training stayers and he had a very good one in High Line, which was a three-year-old in 1969. Recalls Joe: 'High Line was a bit touchy at the stalls, so Henry Candy used to go down to the start with him as they got on well together. He should have won the St Leger but he refused to enter the stalls. Intermezzo won it for Harry Wragg and Ron Hutchinson but every time High Line met Intermezzo he beat him. Another problem with High Line was that he had very big, shallow feet and that put a lot of pressure on his inner soles. For that reason he did most of his racing on good or good to soft ground and ran below his best the only time he raced on a very firm surface. That's why they say that High Line liked it soft. But for his feet, he could have been anything because he had acceleration.'

It was that acceleration that won High Line three successive Jockey Club Cups from 1969 to 1971 and the Geoffrey Freer Stakes in both 1970 and 1971. He has also done very well at stud and there was that remarkable day at York in 1980 when he produced four different winners at various distances. Joe himself won the Acomb Stakes on Cocaine for Jeremy Hindley and the quartet was completed by Master Willie (Benson and Hedges Gold Cup), Shoot A Line (Yorkshire Oaks) and Heighlin (Lonsdale Stakes).

So Joe ended the 1960s with something of a revival. He had topped the century twice, in 1964 and 1965, but the virus at West Ilsley had reduced his total to 68 in 1968. In the circumstances, Joe must have been pleased with his total of 81 the following year. At the end of that season, as he had done for the previous few years, he left to ride in India again. Only this time, it was to turn out to be rather more than just a busman's holiday.

OPPOSITE PAGE:
The 1970 Geoffrey Freer Stakes, Newbury. High Line beats the previous year's St Leger winner, Intermezzo (Ron Hutchinson in the hoops), into third.

Boxed In

Joe was 20 when he and the lightweight jockey, Sammy Millbanks, flew out to ride in Singapore. It was the first time he had ever ridden abroad. Ted Larkin, a highly successful Northern jockey, and Davy Jones, the old gentleman of the weighing-room, were already riding out there. Joe takes up the story:

'Over the Christmas period, when racing moved to Penang, a telegram arrived from Lester Piggott saying he was going to come across from Australia and, if possible, could we fix him up with a few rides? Lester duly arrived, looking very suntanned and rather larger than he is now, weighing about 9st 5lb. We fixed up a few rides for him and, as usual, he rode a winner – to everyone's delight.

'As he was about to leave a few days later, Lester asked Davy Jones if they gave any presents round there for riding winners. On hearing this, Ted Larkin, Sammy Millbanks and myself decided to play a practical joke on Lester. We made out a cheque for roughly £100 from a fictitious owner and gave it to the hall porter to give to Lester when he came in. Lester opened the envelope and was delighted with what he found inside. As he was leaving the next day, he asked Davy Jones if he knew anybody who could cash it for him. Davy said he knew one of the cashiers at the bank and that Lester should take it along there to cash it. We didn't think for one moment that he could cash it because Sammy had written the cheque out on his account which happened to be empty. To our horror, he managed to cash the cheque! At this stage we thought we had better tell Lester what was going on. The reply we got was: "That's your bad luck – I'm off back to England!"

'Within a few days of Lester's departure, Sammy received a letter from the Jockey Club and also from the bank via the Jockey Club – this cheque had been cashed on his account and could he throw some light on it? As there was no money in the account, we all sat together and thought, "God, what do we do now?" Well, the only thing we could do was tell the truth.

Fortunately, the money side was taken care of – Teddy Larkin had quite a lot of money in his account as he was riding most of the winners. So we pushed Sammy Millbanks forward and he had to go to the stewards at Penang racecourse and tell them the whole story. They all had a damned good laugh at our expense!'

After all this excitement, there was the job of riding winners to attend to, but unfortunately Joe met with an accident quite early on. One of his mounts broke its leg and its subsequent fall resulted in Joe damaging a vertebra at the base of his neck. He was told not to ride for a couple of months.

Joe decided during his convalescence to stop at Calcutta on the way home to visit some of the lads who were riding there. He had never been there before and at this stage India was just starting to become really popular among the British jockeys as a place to have a working holiday during the winter. At least that was the idea. Joe's first impressions were rather different: 'I was informed on my arrival that there was to be a big cocktail party that evening in the grounds of the Calcutta Turf Club and I was invited to go along and meet all the lads. I turned up at about 6.30 pm, by which time, the booze being free, everybody had already got rather smashed. The boys were nowhere to be seen but I was told I would find them in the clubhouse where the accommodation was provided for visiting jockeys. Sure enough, there they were – all stretched out on their beds. They had had a few too many, and their discarded dinner jackets, each one attached to a fan blade that was doubling as a rotating hanger, were flying around above them! So that was my first impression of life in India.' Joe stayed in India on that occasion for about ten days and grew to like it.

Harry Carr had spent a lot of time in India and through his father-in-law's connections, Joe acquired a job in Calcutta for a winter's riding in 1960–61. The season starts there in November and lasts until late February/early March. Jimmy Lindley and his wife joined Anne and Joe at the Great Eastern Hotel. Joe had a retainer with the Maharajah of Parlakimedi, but he had been there for scarcely 48 hours when war broke out between Pakistan and India. 'We heard that the troops were marching down to Calcutta,' recalls Joe. 'Anne's father 'phoned up and said, "You know, you'd better get out of there fast because when they start rioting in India, they don't know where to stop." So we left and I was subsequently sued for the first time in my life by the old Maharajah for £300 for breach of contract. It really hurt me to hand over £300 of my hard-earned cash to someone who was hardly in need of it!'

It was about four years later that Joe heard through the grapevine about a very good horse in India called Prince Pradeep, a son of the Aga Khan's 1948 Arc de Triomphe winner, Migoli. Connections were looking for an experienced jockey to ride the colt which apparently was a rather headstrong individual. Recalls Joe: 'The owner of Prince Pradeep was a fellow called Jimmy Gonker (pronounced Gowker) and he came over to England to approach me to go and ride for him that winter. As soon as I saw him, I liked him. He was a very charming fellow and he explained that he had just come into racing. In fact he had become leading owner after only two years and had about a dozen horses in training, with an Arabian trainer called Aziz Mahmoud, most of them named after his children. Little did he know then that in Prince Pradeep, named after his youngest son, he probably had the best horse India had seen for a number of years.'

So off went the Mercer family – Joe's wife, son and nanny – along with newlywed Sammy Millbanks and his wife, to spend the winter of 1964 in India. Racing is a big concern in India and a lot of money changes hands. The Indians are big gamblers, and Jimmy Gonker was one of them. In those days he'd have the

Jimmy Gonker and family.

rupee equivalent of £5,000 on a horse and think nothing of it. 'Mind you, most of the time he'd win,' says Joe. 'Jimmy looked after us terribly well – we had everything we could ever have needed. They gave us a flat at Jahu beach, a beautiful place about ten miles outside Bombay, and a car to get around in. Jimmy was actually involved in gold smuggling and they caught him many years later and confiscated his horses. The whole affair went on for years and years, and when he finally came out of prison, he virtually drank himself to death. It was very sad.'

Joe was impressed with Bombay racecourse when he turned up to ride Prince Pradeep for the first time. 'Bombay is a beautiful racetrack. It is situated very close to the sea wall and there used to be a lovely breeze coming in from the sea in the afternoon. It has an outside tan where you do all the fast work and then on the big grass, which is for racing, it has an inside slow, and an inside fast, as well as another grass track inside that. So that's four tracks in all. The first time I sat on Prince Pradeep, I was told to trot him round and hack him off from a mile and then just canter him back. He was a big, strong horse and the problems began on the way back. He got faster and faster, much faster than I wanted him to go, and the next thing I knew I was a passenger. He just went flat out the whole way round from the five-furlong marker and was that good that when I dismounted I was told he had equalled the five-furlong course record.

'I knew what to expect for the next couple of mornings because he was still running away with me and I knew that it was time to put my foot down. So I decided to fit him with the Citation bridle that I'd brought with me from England, which is a bridle that acts as a restraint on a free running horse. They had never seen one in India before. Well, that was a big help, though it took several days for us to get used to each other. We started off by winning the Guineas trial and then the Guineas itself. I won the 1,000 Guineas too on Mysmita, also owned by Jimmy and trained by Aziz Mahmoud.'

Prince Pradeep went on to win the Derby and the St Leger as well, but Joe, unfortunately, was only a spectator on those occasions. Joe had dismounted after work on a particularly troublesome filly when she lashed out as she was being turned away by her lad. Joe put up his hand to protect his face but there was no protection for his arm, which was broken by the horse's kick. Says Joe: 'Jimmy Gonker was wondering what was going to happen to Prince Pradeep when Anne came up with the obvious answer: "We'll get father out," she said. Harry duly arrived looking a little portly. It took him a few days to get into

shape but as soon as he sat on the horse he said "You're right, Joe, this is one hell of a racehorse!"'

As well as completing the Indian triple crown, Harry also rode Mysmita in the Oaks, in which she was beaten a short head. She was a little temperamental and needed more knowing, and Joe is convinced that he missed out on winning all five classics that year.

Joe preferred a holiday in Barbados the following year but returned to India in 1966–67, 1967–68, 1968–69 and 1969–70. By this time, everyone had joined the bandwagon for Indian winter rides and it was almost like riding in England for the winter. 'From 1966 to 1970 riding with me there were Geoff Lewis, Duncan Keith, Jock Wilson, Taffy Thomas, Bobby Elliott, Paul Cook, Eric Eldin, Frankie Durr and Stan Smith. That was Bombay and in Calcutta there was Bill Rickaby, Chippy Letherbey, Wally Swinburn Senior, Russ Maddock, Eddie Cracknell and Brian Taylor to name but a few. You can see that racing was top class jockey-wise out there. As well as a lucrative time it was a luxurious one – the beautiful weather and the excellent accommodation made it a magnificent holiday for us all, with our wives and children. It was a great way to spend the winter.

'We had a flat where you had your own bearers to look after you. You had your own cook too, so in fact you didn't have to lift a finger and life was extremely pleasant, particularly for the wives. If you wanted to play golf there were numerous golf courses. There was also a beautiful swimming pool called Beach Candy which is quite a famous place in India and became a good meeting place for the families to have a beer, swim and a sunbathe. So all in all, we had a really smashing time!'

On the business side, for the years 1966–70 Joe had a retainer to ride for the trainer Rashid Byramji, who has become one of India's greatest trainers. Later he was to prove himself a great friend to Joe. 'Rashid was exactly the same age as myself, and our wedding anniversary also coincided with his and his wife Dolly's. So Dolly, who was a rather huge lady but very, very jolly, would always put on a very good party on 2 February. I remember when I arrived for the 1968–69 season, and as usual my bearer was sitting on the doorstep waiting for me (you never needed to write to say when you were arriving!), Rashid came round and said he had a surprise for me. So I went down to the track next morning as normal to ride work. You didn't have to start too early, usually at around quarter to seven. At that time it was quite cool and we used to work five or six horses. Well that was when I saw Rashid's surprise – there it was, a big black

OPPOSITE PAGE. ABOVE:
A capacity crowd at Bombay racecourse watches the Indian wonderhorse Prince Pradeep run away with his first Classic.

BELOW:
A delighted Aziz Mahmoud (left) leads in Prince Pradeep after his easy win in the Bombay 2,000 Guineas. Owner Jimmy Gonker is wearing the sunglasses.

horse! Fire Crest had won the Guineas in Madras but was rather headstrong, so we nicknamed him Fiery Fred. After a while, we got on exceptionally well together. He became a star and I won a lot of races on him.'

On several occasions, due to the success of his rides in India, Joe was questioned by the tax authorities back in England about what he had done with all the money he had earned. This needed little explanation. 'I told them I'd spent it. The point was that the Bank of England wouldn't change the rupees and the Bank of India wouldn't change them for you either, or let them out of the country, so it was quite stupid to even think about bringing the money home because it was useless. So we spent a lot of it on ourselves out there, simply having a damned good time, and we also brought home a few items such as carpets and things like that.'

But in 1970 the money Joe earned in India resulted in a terrible experience. 'As I was leaving for home on 22 February, I was arrested at Bombay Airport, Santa Cruz. They asked if I had anything to declare, and like a bloody idiot I said, "No," not thinking that, unlike in England where you can buy what you like and take it out of the country, it was illegal to take anything of value out of India with you. I was arrested on the spot. I had bought a lot of stuff, a few valuable items among which were two good diamonds in my pocket. I had pooled all my resources to buy them, planning to have them made up into something special for my wife or perhaps to sell one and make some money to get something out of my winter riding for a change.

'The authorities thought differently and were not interested in any of my explanations. They held me overnight and I had no idea in those days of how to get a solicitor, particularly at night and in India, as it was by then around 10.00 pm. They refused to allow me to contact my trainer, Rashid Byramji, but luckily for me Rashid had heard of my plight and sent me a lawyer, a Mr Mauji, who arranged bail. I was let out but they confiscated my passport. I was allowed to continue riding.

'During this time, my lawyer and various other influential people tried to get a Court Order that would somehow allow me to get out of the country. It appeared that there was one judge, whom they nicknamed "The Hangman", who often gave six months in prison to anyone he wanted to make an example of. By this time I was worried to death and a nervous wreck. After two or three weeks my solicitors organised a preview Court hearing and it was there, to our horror, that the very judge we did not want decided to take on my case!

'The trial date was decided, with this judge presiding. Of course, the press were having a field day. I was accused of smuggling "diamonds" – there were actually only two but not being specific made it sound a very big business. I was only taking or, as they put it, smuggling what I had bought with my own money, not what I had heard that some of the big ring smugglers did.

'I was in the dock for only a few minutes before I was found guilty and sentenced to three months' imprisonment in Poona. Classified a Grade 1 prisoner, I realised I was a condemned criminal and was led away with a police escort. It's when they take you away after you've heard your sentence that you first realise you're in trouble.

'They allowed Rashid and his wife Dolly to walk a few yards with me, where they helped me to fill in a form with my date of birth, religion and all that jazz. They took my watch, my lucky charms and my St Christopher that I wear around my neck, for which I signed. By now I was almost in tears and I said goodbye and was taken down below the Court to a huge prison cell where all the other convicted people were sitting waiting for the Black Maria to take them away. The stench down there was terrible and I began to feel really scared.

'In the afternoon we were hustled into a sort of barred truck and were driven to the local Bombay prison to stay overnight. We were marched in, told to strip off our clothes and were issued with so-called prison clothes, a baggy flannel get-up, and then they proceeded to cut off all our hair. I just sat there with my nerves on edge and near me was another guy who was English, and we got together and confided in each other. They shaved our heads completely – the Yul Brynner style! – which does not suit nine out of ten people, I can assure you. I had not much to shave off, but off it came all the same! We were then given a blanket and followed the other prisoners into a huge dormitory with no beds where we slept on the floor. I didn't sleep a wink. I organised it so that I lay next to the Englishman and asked, "What are you in for?" He answered "Smuggling," and I said, "So am I." He said, "I guessed that, I got seven years." "What for, smuggling diamonds?" I was so shocked. "Working for an organisation where some get through and some don't" he replied. "Luck of the game, old boy." I told him I got three months for smuggling two diamonds and he explained that they got diamonds into Bombay, where they fetched a very high price.

'The next morning, we were served porridge and bread. Luckily for me I had made friends while riding for the Sampat family, a father and three sons. They were punters, professional gamblers, who had known more about what was cooking on the course than I did. They had plenty of local influence and bribed their way into the prison to visit me. They fixed it so that I got a decent cell in the grounds of the local prison in Bombay. They were a lifesaver, bringing me food and having a daily chat, which maintained my morale.

'They discovered, through the grapevine, that I was due to be moved to Poona jail together with a trainload of other prisoners. By this time, I was being accorded the rights of a first class prisoner. The Sampats came to the station and again bribed the guard to let me travel with them in a normal compartment instead of in the truck-train. It was a long journey to Poona, at least one and a half hours, but they stayed with me until we arrived at the prison and, once I was there, things did not look quite so bad. I was ushered in to see the Governor, who told me to take things as they came. "You won't find it too difficult," he declared.

'By now, thanks to the Sampats, I had acquired some personal belongings and a toothbrush, a T-shirt and shorts. I was shown to my prison block which faced another one 30 yards away. We had a large cell each and they were quite airy and at least had some light. In the compound, a lot of people were sitting around having tea on a verandah and they asked me to join them there overlooking the grounds. They all spoke good English and practically all the guys in that block had something in common – they were all hardened villains! I cannot recollect all their names but I was there in Poona for three weeks and everyone was helpful, showing me the ropes and advising me of my rights – it was permitted, for example, to have food sent in. Again I was lucky. Rashid's father lived in Poona, running a big stud there, and my food was sent in every morning, eggs, fish and many other things – very good food that would form my lunch and evening meal, with any leftovers making the next day's breakfast. As for cigarettes, no problem. I got the warder to collect money from Rashid's father and bring me packets and other bits and pieces when I wanted them.

'A few days after settling in I asked what they did all day. They had, it appeared, various jobs such as weaving. The Governor asked me what I could do and I answered, looking at the garden, that I was not bad at gardening. Before I knew it, I was appointed gardener with several prisoners under me as helpers. I asked for secateurs, which duly arrived. The garden was out of hand and the roses unpruned. I chopped them down according to the English method. They were horrified but, in such a warm climate, just as I had promised in a week they were growing – thank heavens! – like wildfire. This, together with walking as much as possible round the block, kept me fit. I was also eating well and was always out in the sun wearing only shorts, so I had a real tan – more black than tan – and I looked like a native. At five o'clock you went to have your shower and, because of the heat, the water was warm.

'It was at around 6.30 pm that you came down to earth and realised that you were in prison, when you heard the clang of the doors and the locks turning. That was it and you were left with your candle. In my cell, I had company every night – a little family of mongooses. I had left a plate of food on the floor one night and I heard rattling and something devouring my leftovers. So I left some every night and they came at dusk and brought their family with them. They were really interesting to watch – it was like a nature programme on television. It helped to pass the time and was something to think about, a bit of excitement in the day. It was amazing how I looked forward to these little family visits. If they were a bit late, it disturbed me and I used to wonder what the hell had happened.'

Joe served 20 days of his three-month prison sentence in Poona jail. He was there from 26 March until 15 April, ironically also the date of his wife Anne's birthday. The case had eventually passed to the High Court and a deal was struck whereby he was allowed to leave the country provided he paid his fines within seven days of being released from prison.

Dolly and Rashid Byramji were waiting for Joe when he was let out and immediately whisked him off to Rashid's father's nearby stud farm where he was able to have a proper wash and shave. They then drove him to Bombay to stay in a hotel for the night.

'It was all up to the solicitors,' says Joe. 'Once in Bombay I saw the top man in the Inland Revenue office. Again, it was a case of *who* you knew rather than *what* you knew. Putu Sing, a jockey, was a personal friend of this man's and I got to meet him the following morning instead of having to wait at least a week, which I would have had to have done in normal circumstances. The Inland Revenue officer was another charming fellow who had been educated in England. He didn't go into any details, all he said was that if I returned that afternoon at four o'clock with a certain sum of money, my passport would be stamped.

'Rashid and Dolly took me to the bank and we got it all fixed for me to leave the country the following day. I decided to leave the way I had arrived, that is, first class, and they all came to say farewell at the airport. The red carpet was laid out and it was straight through customs and on to the plane where champagne had been especially laid on. They had organised everything and it was quite an emotional scene.'

Meanwhile, Anne Mercer had been through quite an ordeal herself at home. 'I heard of Joe's arrest when we thought he was on his way home and were all getting ready to fetch him from the airport with his favourite meal already prepared. The 'phone rang and a strange voice asked, "What's it like to have a jailbird for a husband?" I found out later that this had been someone from a daily newspaper. At the time, I had a friend staying with me and I asked her to answer any calls after this shock. Friends then started to ring and you certainly find out who your friends are when something like that happens. I heard no news of Joe until Mr Byramji rang and said that he had seen him, and that he was the best he could be and that he sent his love. I simply went numb and couldn't believe it wasn't a bad dream.

'Not only was I worried and unable to sleep or to think of anything else, but the children were also upset daily. One would not believe how cruel and beastly children can be to each other. Our eldest son, Henry, then ten years old, was a weekly boarder at our local school and they ribbed him unmercifully, calling him the jailbird's son and every other name you could think of to humiliate and hurt the boy. I took him away for a week, hoping things would calm down while he was away. I suppose they did, as he was willing to face them again but he was upset deep down and it took a long time for him to get over it. Although he said very little I knew – what mother would not? My daughter was too young to notice, she only kept asking, "When is Daddy coming home?"

'Jakie Astor used to ring me at least once a week to tell me how things were progressing. Of course I wanted to go out there but was told I would only add to the complications and would almost certainly be arrested as well. At last Joe was allowed to 'phone – one call – and he said, "For heaven's sake do not come out. Pay no attention to what anyone says in the way of what you should or should not do. Do nothing and don't come out, wait at home." He said he would only have more to worry about if I even contemplated coming and that was that.

'As well as Jakie Astor the British Embassy were very helpful and kind to me. At least twice a week I had a call from them saying, "Don't worry, everything is all right, he will be home soon." I will always be thankful to them, although I felt I was living in a vacuum. I imagined all that could happen or go wrong or an accident through other prisoners. Television films showing prisons in very civilised countries, even our own, certainly help your imagination run away with you. It was a nightmare I never want to go through again.

'I went to stay for a few days with my mother and father at Newmarket and a call came from Joe to tell me he was out at last and would be home in a few days. He gave me the flight number and time and I was such a nervous wreck I did not want even to drive on my own. I took a friend with me. When I saw him I just burst into tears. No excuse or particular reason, it just happened. He looked so frail I just thought, "What have they done to him?" His head had been shaved and he looked just as you imagine someone would look who had just come out of prison. I was no help – I kept on crying and was useless for the rest of the day. We talked and talked and eventually seemed to cope with everything. The press were very good but it was harrowing and never seemed to end.'

The Mercers can now think back and smile about it all. As Joe says, 'Considering it was prison, it really wasn't so bad and of course I have to thank all my friends out there for that. In many ways it didn't do me any harm. I used to be a bit hot-tempered and it cooled me down.

'I remember one very awkward individual who was one of the head stewards at Bombay. His name was Solly Captain and he really had it in for me. One day somebody had objected to me and we were called in after the race to watch the stewards play with their tiny model horses in an attempt to reconstruct what had happened. After I had stated my case, they let me keep the race, but I was still quite angry as I stalked off to mount my horse for the next race. Then Solly Captain came out shouting "Mercer, Mercer!" I just carried on walking round and he continued to shout my name. Finally, I turned round and said "It's Mr Mercer to you, and when I get off this one you can have my f . . . ing licence!" Sure enough, after the race, I stormed into his office and slung it at him. Rashid pleaded with me to apologise, and after a while, for his sake, I did.

'I remember him saying to me when they put me in prison: "You'll never, ever get a licence to ride in this country again!" I saw him in 1985 on the July course at Newmarket, walked up to him, tapped him on the shoulder and said: "Hello Solly Captain, you're still alive then!" He turned round and said, "It's you!" "Yes," I replied, "and still riding strong." He was still wearing the same suit I think.'

OVERLEAF:
The taste of freedom. Out riding work a million miles from Poona jail.

Joe's friends have invited him back to India on many occasions since his disastrous experience there, but so far he has never returned. He has received assurances that there would be no trouble if he was to pass through Indian Customs again, but the memory of his adventure obviously still haunts him. 'I still have a lot of good friends out there,' he says, 'and it would be nice to see them again. Perhaps one day I'll go back.'

The Brigadier Gerard Years

When Joe arrived back in England from Bombay, the first thing he wanted to do was to go to West Ilsley and ride work. Jakie Astor was the first to get in touch with him and advised him to go off and have a week's rest. Joe replied that he felt as fit as a fiddle and was raring to go. But Jakie said, 'I don't mean it like that, Joe, there's been a bit of a problem in the yard with Brook Holliday's horses, especially Highest Hopes.'

Highest Hopes was a promising three-year-old daughter of Hethersett who had won her only start as a two-year-old. Unfortunately for Joe, while he had been away his pal Jimmy Lindley had been riding out and had won the Ascot 1,000 Guineas Trial and the Fred Darling Stakes at Newbury on her. As a result, Highest Hopes was to start joint favourite for the Newmarket classic with Peter Walwyn's Humble Duty.

'Obviously, Major Holliday didn't want me to ride her, so I did what Jakie Astor suggested and took a few days off,' Joe recalls. 'My first winning ride for the stable was on Crescent Dart, who won her maiden at Bath. We had a bad draw but she was never headed and obviously I hadn't lost any of my flair at that track.' At that time, and throughout his career in fact, Joe was the jockey to follow at Bath. He recorded 205 wins there, a total that was bettered only by his score of 226 at Newmarket.

Highest Hopes has a top class field well strung out as she wins the Prix Vermeille at Longchamp with something to spare.

The best filly in Europe. That's Highest Hopes as she is led in after winning the Prix Vermeille. Note the prominence of the blood vessels after her exertions.

In the event Humble Duty won the 1,000 Guineas as Highest Hopes inexplicably tailed off. A subsequent dope test proved negative, and nobody really knows what went wrong. 'The thing about Highest Hopes' explains Joe, 'was that she was very "shouldery" and needed some give in the ground. She couldn't even walk when she came out of her box in the mornings and would have fallen over if you'd pushed her. Like High Line, she lived on phenylbutazone to relieve the pain. But she was brilliant on the track, she really flowed.' Highest Hopes, with Joe back up, soon put the Guineas disappointment behind her when she ran second to Sweet Mimosa in the Prix de Diane, the French Oaks at Chantilly. A victory in the Prix Eugene Adam at Saint-

Cloud followed before she was beaten by Lupe in the Yorkshire Oaks. But in her greatest triumph, she got her revenge on both Sweet Mimosa and Lupe in the semi-classic Prix Vermeille at Longchamp in September, accounting for 'the best field of three-year-old fillies assembled in Europe in 1970, and probably the world too,' according to *Racehorses of 1970*. Joe rode a particularly inspired race that day, sending his mount on after turning into the straight and never allowing any rivals to get in a blow.

Back at the beginning of the season, on Joe's first morning riding work, he sat on Brigadier Gerard for the first time, and one of racing's most celebrated partnerships began. As winner of 17 of his 18 starts, Brigadier Gerard was, quite simply, one of the best horses ever to have raced in Britain. He won Group One races from six furlongs to a mile and a half and is arguably the greatest miler of all time. He was a public idol in the early 1970s, capturing everybody's imagination and admiration. To give younger readers an idea of just how good he was, imagine the 'race of the century', say over a mile and a quarter at Ascot, with the line-up consisting of the Brigadier, Dancing Brave, El Gran Senor, Mill Reef, Nijinsky, Pebbles and Sir Ivor. According to *Timeform's Racehorses* annuals, whose ratings are far more compelling than any argument, the Brigadier would win – with a bit to spare! In *Timeform*'s 40 years of rating racehorses only one horse, Sea-Bird II, has ever been rated higher (145) than Brigadier Gerard (144).

'The very first time I heard about Brigadier Gerard was from Bobby Elliott. Bobby, who is a great friend of mine, was riding work for Dick Hern and to keep me amused in prison he used to drop me lines telling me how the horses were getting on. "You'd better hurry up and come back," he wrote, "because we have some very good two-year-olds and one in particular could be a bit special." '

The lads all laughed when Joe sat on Brigadier Gerard that morning. Bobby Elliott was riding behind. 'You watch the old bugger,' he said, 'because he can come round a bit quick. He's already got rid of me and Jimmy Lindley and everybody else who's ridden him for the first time.'

Joe, understandably, was a little wary. 'We had a trot, an amble up the road, and the horse never moved. Then I went across to the canter and about 20 yards before I got there, the horse just whipped around and the next thing I knew I was on my backside looking up at him! The horse looked down, and his expression said "Well, I've put you in your place as well, boy, now you can get back on." From that point we had no problems.

The Brigadier was always a nice horse to sit on. He was a beautiful mover and a great character. He used to give his lead horse three or four lengths' start and once he had a neck up on him he thought he had done enough. He would never pulverise any of his working companions.'

Eventually, Dick Hern decided to run Brigadier Gerard in the Berkshire Stakes at Newbury on 24 June 1970. There were only four other runners in the race and they had all won before. Brigadier Gerard started the joint outsider at 100–7. The runners didn't hang about and the newcomer was soon outpaced. About halfway, though, he began to make a little progress and then the whole race changed as he shifted gear and came from last to first to win by five lengths, going away. Clearly the colt had tremendous potential.

Brigadier Gerard was bred and owned by the leading racing journalist, John Hislop, in partnership with his wife, Jean. He wasn't bred to be anything special. His dam, La Paiva, who was by the 1946 French Derby winner, Prince Chevalier, failed to win. His sire was Queen Hussar who was yet to produce anything of note and was really little more than a top class mile handicapper in his racing days. True, he won the 1963 Sussex Stakes, but in those days the race carried nothing like the prestige that it does today.

Brigadier Gerard had come out of his Newbury race so well that John Hislop and Dick Hern decided to run him in the Champagne Stakes at Salisbury eight days later. The way that the Brigadier was to win this race made his connections realise that he was going to be a very good racehorse. 'There was some barging in the middle which left the Brigadier with plenty to do. I had to ease him up off the fence and come round and, to his credit, he charged to the front and won by four lengths.'

Brigadier Gerard was then given a long rest because Buster Haslam, Dick Hern's travelling head lad, told John Hislop that he had seen the horse weaving when he got back from Salisbury. Hislop wanted to give his horse the time to realise he wasn't going to run every week. The Brigadier came back and trotted up in the Washington Singer Stakes at Newbury before he won the Middle Park Stakes at Newmarket very easily from Mummy's Pet, Swing Easy and Fireside Chat, who were to prove themselves top sprinters the following year. Brigadier Gerard was allotted 9st 5lb in the Free Handicap behind My Swallow (9st 7lb), and Mill Reef (9st 6lb).

At the end of 1970, Sir Gordon Richards, who had taken up training at Marlborough in 1955, announced his retirement from training and took up a new position as racing manager to Sir Michael Sobell and Lady Beaverbrook. A little earlier, Sobell had bought the West Ilsley stables from Jakie Astor. Sobell had planned for Sir Gordon to continue training at West Ilsley but Jakie had sold only on the condition that Dick Hern and Joe Mercer remained as trainer and jockey. As a consequence, all the Sobell- and Beaverbrook-owned horses were moved to West Ilsley to start the 1971 season. Reflects Joe: 'As well as inheriting some nice horses that improved the quality of the yard, we also got several of Sir Gordon's staff, including Brian Proctor.'

So there was every reason to be optimistic at the beginning of 1971. Brigadier Gerard had also wintered very well. 'I used to make it a regular habit, in order to get fit, to start riding probably a month before racing. Riding two lots and sweeping up the yard and that sort of thing in between all added to my fitness. I was able to keep an eye on the Brigadier and I thought he looked exceptionally well. He looked magnificent and as big as a bull when I first saw him at the end of February. Our horses had in fact all wintered well and we had a tremendous start to the season.'

One of these horses was Duration, who was assisting the Brigadier in his work. Duration had needed the run on his appearance but had won his next start at Warwick. Leading up to the Guineas, for which there would be no preparatory race for the Brigadier, the four-year-old Duration worked with Brigadier Gerard at level weights. That morning in the pouring rain, Joe had on his mackintosh bottoms and was also wearing a very heavy suede jacket which he used a lot when riding out because it was lined and very warm. 'I had ridden three bits of work prior to the Brigadier and my jacket was getting pretty soggy and the water was coming through. The horse worked very well and we were very pleased with him. I had to go racing that day so I popped back home and jumped on the scales. To my amazement, they showed 9st 5lb. I took the jacket off and worked out that with all the water it had soaked up, it weighed 8lb or 9lb. So obviously the horse's work that morning had been even better than we'd all thought!'

The big day arrived. The race before the 2,000 Guineas was an apprentice race over the Rowley Mile in which the lead horse, Duration, was performing. Obviously, the better he ran, the more of a boost there would be for Brigadier Gerard and, as Joe recalls, 'Naturally, everybody in the yard had a few bob on the Brigadier plus a few bob on Duration. I actually went into the stands with my binoculars and followed Duration in the race. I saw the old horse's face appear under Laurie Davis, and he came out of the dip virtually on his own to win very easily by five lengths!'

'When Laurie came in, the Guv'nor walked in with a broad smile and said: "Well done. Don't forget to weigh in". As we watched the boy jump on the scales I said to Dick, "Well, that's great for us, Dick, isn't it?" "Absolutely, bloody marvellous!" he replied. So we went out there with terrific confidence.'

There were only six runners in the Guineas and most people thought the race would develop into a duel between My Swallow and Mill Reef. Both had won their warm-up races impressively, the Usher Stakes at Kempton and the Greenham Stakes at Newbury respectively. The pair had met in the Prix Robert Papin the previous autumn, when the verdict had gone to My Swallow by a short head, and for much of the winter discussion between racing enthusiasts had centred around their rematch. The betting reflected this, with Mill Reef starting favourite at 6–4 and My Swallow at 2–1. The Brigadier was an 11–2 chance and the only other runner seriously supported was Nijinsky's brother Minsky at 15–2, who had already won the Gladness and Tetrarch Stakes for Vincent O'Brien and Lester Piggott.

Joe recounts how the race was run: 'I knew that Frankie Durr would bounce My Swallow out of the gate and let him bowl along and that Geoff Lewis would just tuck in behind on Mill Reef. I thought the thing to do was just to sit in behind them both and get a lead. They played beautifully into my hands – I wouldn't say they jumped off and cut each other's throats, but they went at a hell of a lick and it was quite apparent, from where I sat just behind them with about two and a bit to go, that there was nobody going better than myself. When I asked the old horse to pick up and do a bit, my God did he pick up! We just went sailing by them and that was the end of that. He was a machine.'

The Brigadier crossed the line three lengths in front of Mill Reef, who had My Swallow threequarters of a length behind in third. Interestingly, Brigadier Gerard picked up £27,283.40 for his win compared to £107,145 won by Dancing Brave 15 years later.

Brigadier Gerard didn't run in the Derby. John Hislop made the decision in his own mind when walking down from the stand to the unsaddling enclosure after his Guineas win. He felt that the horse's speed had been the main factor in that victory. In his book *The Brigadier*, he gives his other reasons:

'Besides this, he was still immature and a hard race in the Derby might have finished him off at this stage of his racing

career, as it has done so many Derby contestants in the past, both winners and losers. Always, we had considered the Brigadier as unlikely to reach his best until he was four, and I did not wish to prejudice his future. Furthermore, though he did not become unbalanced during the descent into the Dip, he was seen to much greater advantage as he breasted the rising ground, which was a clear indication that Epsom, with its steep gradients, would be a far from ideal course for him.' On hearing about this decision, Hislop quotes Joe as saying: 'I'm delighted. The course wouldn't suit him and you might jar him up.' The fact that Brigadier Gerard was able to win 12 of his subsequent 13 races suggests that the policy paid off handsomely.

So the Brigadier's next race was the St James's Palace Stakes at Royal Ascot. That year there had been so much rain that the course was almost waterlogged. This was not in the Brigadier's favour. As Joe says, 'The Brigadier always preferred good to fast

Brigadier Gerard is out on his own as he pulverises both Mill Reef and My Swallow in the 1971 2,000 Guineas. This was to become a familiar sight.

93

ground – he bounced off fast ground. That day I came very close to defeat because Lester Piggott was on a soft ground specialist in Sparkler.' Lester nearly stole the race that day in his attempt to make all the running. The Brigadier had lost his action when pulled out to challenge and had a lot of ground to make up on Sparkler. It looked as though he was going to get beaten for the first time. John Hislop describes what happened next:

'Joe Mercer is a magnificent jockey at any time, but in times of stress he is superb and in the St James's Palace Stakes he excelled himself. Keeping the Brigadier perfectly balanced, which was no mean task in such going, he encouraged him with hands, heels and the swing of his whip; he gave him a tap, and when the horse responded did not touch him again, knowing that he was doing his utmost and would only resent further pressure.'

With every stride the gap was narrowed and Joe forced the Brigadier up to catch and beat Sparkler a head. Though he had had a hard race, the Brigadier's next three wins could not have been more impressive. He won the Sussex Stakes at Goodwood, the Goodwood Mile and the Queen Elizabeth II Stakes at Ascot by a staggering aggregate of 23 lengths. 'In those cases,' recalls Joe, 'he virtually took off. He was a horse you never thought about getting beaten on. There was no set pattern of riding him, you could ride him whichever way you liked. As with all good horses, there's not a lot you had to do on him really.'

Apart from the Guineas, Joe believes the Brigadier's greatest triumph that year was the Champion Stakes in October. The weather seemed to go against him and it was one of those Newmarket meetings where the rain never seemed to stop. It just came down cats and dogs the whole of the night before and the whole day right up until the race. 'The Brigadier ran a marvellous race to win that day, I thought. He was tackling a mile and a quarter for the first time and in very testing ground. I kicked for home just coming down the hill and he went clear. It was apparent to all the people in the stands, with about 100 yards to go, that he was feeling the ground a bit and Rarity, ridden by Pat Eddery, came with a very late, strong challenge and only just failed to get up. I only held on by a cat's whisker and he came in to a fantastic ovation. By the end of his three-year-old career he was unbeaten in ten races.'

Ever since Brigader Gerard had beaten Mill Reef in the Guineas, the racing world had been waiting for a rematch between the two great colts. While the Brigadier had confirmed that he was an outstanding miler, undoubtedly the best seen for years, Mill Reef had tackled middle distances. He won the Derby

OPPOSITE PAGE:
In the paddock before the 1971 Champion Stakes a rain-lashed Mercer contemplates the task facing the unbeaten Brigadier.

before beating France's best four-year-old, Caro, by four lengths in the Eclipse Stakes. After a six-length triumph in the King George he was rested until the Prix de l'Arc de Triomphe.

Dick Hern and Joe Mercer also had a fancied runner in the Arc that year in Lady Beaverbrook's Royalty. Royalty, a brown son of Relko, had a most uncharacteristic preparation for the Arc but came to the race unbeaten in his six races as a three-year-old. He had started off by winning his maiden at Newmarket before succeeding in minor races at Lingfield and Kempton. The only time he took on very useful company was in winning the Warren Stakes at Goodwood in July and his Arc preparation had been completed in the three-runner North Yorkshire Stakes at Redcar, of all places. He ran an excellent race in the Arc, finishing six lengths sixth to Mill Reef after being baulked early in the race, and in fact finished lame. He was the second three-year-old colt home. Joe reflects: 'Royalty was a good horse. To run sixth in the Arc after breaking down half a mile out was a tremendous effort. He was unable to race again.' So just how good Royalty really was will never be known.

But Dick Hern and Joe Mercer had every reason to be satisfied with their visits to France that year. The Coventry Stakes winner, Sun Prince, owned by Sir Michael Sobell, took the Prix Robert Papin at Maisons-Laffitte and the smart colt Colum was successful in the mile-and-a-quarter Prix Ridgway at Deauville. As a four-year-old he also won at Saint-Cloud the following May. Adds Joe: 'We had three good two-year-olds in 1971 that looked like making a name for themselves: Sallust, Sun Prince and Rampage. Of the three, I thought Rampage, owned by Lady Beaverbrook, was the best. But after winning the Champagne at Salisbury he dropped dead under me at Ascot next time out. They never could find out the cause of death.'

At the start of the 1972 campaign, John Hislop had decided on a plan of action for Brigadier Gerard. From three to four the Brigadier had matured. He looked a bigger horse and although his racing weight was more or less the same throughout, he had become a lot more muscular. The 2,000 Guineas was the last race Brigadier Gerard started at odds against. He was made 4–1 on to beat a modest field in the Lockinge Stakes at Newbury and was never in any danger when beating Grey Mirage. Joe then gave him a very easy race when he followed up in the Westbury Stakes at Sandown by a comfortable half-length from Ballyhot. Next stop was Royal Ascot and the Prince of Wales' Stakes.

One of the greatest and most emotional receptions given to any horse and rider in recent years was accorded to Brigadier

Gerard and Joe Mercer after the Prince of Wales' Stakes at Ascot in 1972. It was as much of a tribute to the jockey as to the popularity of the horse. Two days earlier, on the Sunday, Joe had been in a 'plane crash in which the pilot, Graham Cameron, was killed, just after taking off from Newbury racecourse for a flight to Belgium. Graham Cameron was not only a regular pilot for Joe and Jimmy Lindley, but a personal friend in whom they had complete confidence. Joe was in the first of two 'planes to take off for the same destination and, when it had reached approximately 100 feet, it suddenly swung to the left and dived into a swamp alongside the mile starting point. Joe was sitting in the middle of the 'plane between trainer Bill Marshall and his wife, Pam, but not having fastened his seat belt, he was able to bolt out of the back door which had been flung open by the force of the crash. He quickly returned to free the other passengers but the pilot was dead at the controls. Bill Marshall and the other two passengers

Lucky to be alive. Joe recuperates with his youngest son, Joseph, after the horrific 'plane crash at Newbury.

were saved before the plane caught fire and exploded. Joe was badly bruised and shaken but was detained for no more than a couple of hours in hospital. He was determined to ride the Brigadier on the Tuesday but Jimmy Lindley was standing by in case he was not fit.

With such an important race coming up two days later, many owners would have decided there and then that it would be better if Joe did not ride the Brigadier. John and Jean Hislop took another view. They decided that as no other jockey had ever ridden their horse in a race, they did not want the partnership broken up if it was at all possible to keep it intact. The horse was an easy ride, except that he tended to pull rather strongly, and he did not have a lot to beat. They left the decision entirely up to Joe and, if he felt fit enough, he was to take the ride.

On the Tuesday morning, at West Ilsley, after a strong work out, Joe announced that he was fit enough to take the ride in the Prince of Wales' Stakes at Ascot that afternoon. Before they entered the starting stalls, the starter asked 'How are you feeling, Joe?' The reply came: 'I'm feeling fine now, but I won't be in five minutes' time.' Brigadier Gerard proceeded to beat the subsequent Irish Sweeps Derby winner, Steel Pulse, five lengths and broke the course record for one and a quarter miles, although he lost about four lengths coming out of the stalls. Joe is sure that the horse sensed he was below par that afternoon and, for the first time in a race, the Brigadier didn't pull his jockey's arms out. In fact he made the rider's task very simple and, as Joe described afterwards, did it all himself.

But the ordeal at Newbury had taken more out of Joe than he had realised. He was near to collapse as he was led through the cheering crowd who wanted to show their appreciation of his courage. He didn't ride again at the meeting – Jimmy Lindley substituted to win the St James's Palace Stakes on Sun Prince – and it was another week before he felt well enough to resume riding.

The Eclipse Stakes at Sandown on 8 July was looked upon by all racegoers, and in particular by the media, as the 'race of the century' in anticipation of both the Brigadier and Mill Reef meeting again. But it was never to happen. Mill Reef had hacked up on his reappearance in the Prix Ganay but had then come close to defeat at the hands of Homeric in the Coronation Cup at Epsom. Homeric, owned by Sir Michael Sobell, had won the Lingfield Derby trial for Dick Hern and Joe Mercer in 1971 and ended the season with a neck second to Athens Wood in the St Leger. He was, therefore, well established in the top flight but he

The race that never was. The Brigadier fails to impress in beating a modest field on testing ground in the 1972 Eclipse Stakes.

certainly wasn't entitled to run Mill Reef to a neck, even under a vintage ride from Joe in the Coronation Cup, as he in fact did. Later Mill Reef was found to be sickening for a virus and had clearly not been himself. After that Ian Balding could not get him right. Mill Reef was being prepared for the Arc when he broke a leg on the gallops in August and the Coronation Cup turned out to be his last race.

As for the Eclipse, it was probably just as well that a super fit Mill Reef (who acted well in the soft) was an absentee. Due to incessant rain, the ground came up very soft and it was only because of the sub-standard quality of the opposition that connections decided that the Brigadier should run. He didn't impress in beating Gold Rod a length.

When the King George VI and Queen Elizabeth Stakes, sponsored for the first time by the De Beers diamond company, was announced as the next race for the wonder horse, it gave anybody interested in racing a new topic to talk about. Would Brigadier Gerard get a mile and a half? Sir Gordon Richards, talking to Claude Duval in *The Sun*, said at the time: 'Brigadier Gerard is one of the finest horses of all time. His unbeaten record proves this. He's got such guts that he just won't be beaten. For a horse to be called great, he must be unbeaten. That's why Ribot

99

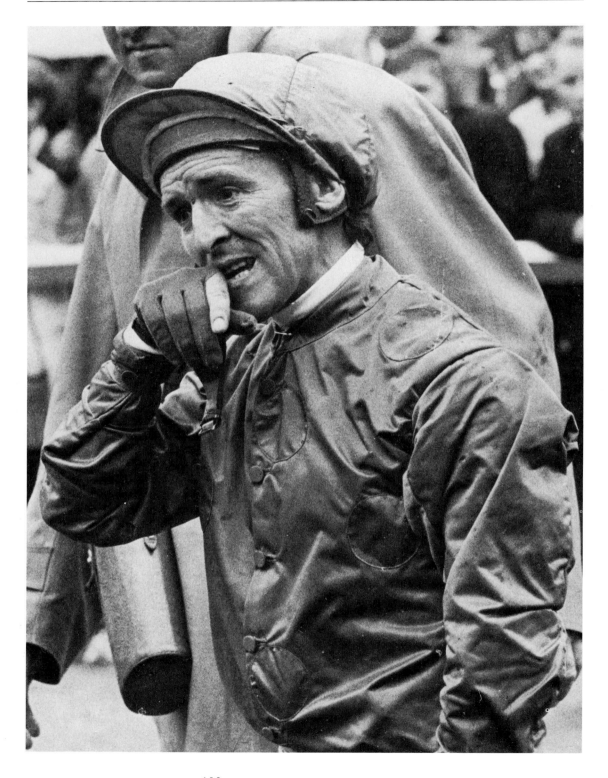

and Bahram were so outstanding. But if Brigadier Gerard does win the King George, we must certainly put him in this bracket. Unbeaten horses fascinate me. We never really know just how great they are. I believe Brigadier Gerard will get one and a half miles for the first time. He's got such a wonderful temperament.'

On the day of the race Joe and Anne were negotiating for a 112-acre farm a few miles outside Newbury. 'We could just about afford it, particularly if the Brigadier was to win that day. We commissioned a local agent to go to bid for us at the sale of Cold Ash Farm.' Brigadier Gerard's opposition in the King George included the top French colt Riverman, winner of the French 2,000 Guineas, the Irish Sweeps Derby winner Steel Pulse, the unbeaten Italian Derby winner Gay Lussac, and the very smart stayer Parnell, winner of the 1971 Irish St Leger. Joe describes the race.

'Several jockeys in the race thought I would not get the trip and they held the same opinion about Riverman. Therefore, they set a very fast pace in the hope of outstaying us. My horse moved beautifully and, entering the straight, I only had Parnell in front of me. As we moved smoothly into the lead, the Brigadier edged right towards the far rails, cutting across the path being followed

OPPOSITE PAGE:
The exhaustion shows after the Brigadier's workmanlike win at Sandown.

Down on the farm. Joe with his young helpers Sarah and Joseph.

by Parnell and Willie Carson. As I was being congratulated by the other jockeys on pulling up, Willie came past, calling, "You will lose it." When they announced that there was to be an inquiry, I was terrified and didn't know whether I had won or not. Willie was still teasing me as we went to weigh in. We were then called into the stewards' room and I was trembling at the knees as I gave my explanation. Watching the replay, I thought Willie's performance deserved an Oscar. We were told to wait outside as is the normal practice. While we waited Willie said, "You're sure to lose," and I said, "Shut up, Willie" – he can get your back up a bit in instances like that. Although I was convinced I had not interfered with Parnell in the least, it was a very worrying ten minutes before the announcement that the placings would remain unaltered was made.'

On the way home, the Mercers stopped off for a drink with friends and Joe took the opportunity, to 'phone the estate agent. After congratulating Joe, he told him that he had acquired Cold Ash Farm, where the Mercers still live today. 'I was delighted. The Brigadier had helped pay for a substantial portion of the farm and put the seal on a perfect day. I ought to have called it Brigadier Gerard Farm but I didn't think it sounded quite right.'

1972 was a particularly successful year for Joe. As well as the immortal Brigadier, the stable also housed another very good miler in the form of Sallust, a chestnut son of Pall Mall, owned by Sir Michael Sobell. 'The first time Sallust ran he finished about last and was a big disappointment. So we worked him in blinkers and he went so fast that he sustained sore shins and couldn't run again for weeks.' Sallust ended the season a smart two-year-old, gaining his most important win in the Richmond Stakes. He ran in the Kempton 2,000 Guineas trial on his first start at three, but disappointed after sweating up badly. But later it transpired he had a virus and he missed the Classics. Sallust wasn't seen out again until Derby Day at Epsom when he won the Diomed Stakes. He was to win all four of his remaining outings: the Prix de la Porte Maillot at Longchamp; the Sussex Stakes and Goodwood Mile; and the Prix du Moulin de Longchamp, and ended the season as the champion three-year-old miler of Europe.

In the Sussex Stakes, there was a tremendous tussle between Willie Carson on the 2,000 Guineas winner, High Top, and Joe on Sallust. They were locked in battle for the last two furlongs and there was only a head in it as Sallust broke the course record. Sallust also lowered the Longchamp mile record in the Moulin in holding off a determined challenge from Lyphard.

The track record was also to fall at York in August with the inaugural running of the Benson and Hedges Gold Cup, Brigadier Gerard's next race after the King George. Although the Brigadier broke the previous record himself, the unthinkable happened and he went down by three lengths to the Derby winner, Roberto, in one of the great upsets of post-war racing. It was his first defeat in 16 starts. The winner was ridden by Braulio Baeza, a Panamanian whom owner John Galbraith and trainer Vincent O'Brien had brought over from America, as Lester Piggott, who had won the Derby on Roberto, preferred to ride Rheingold, whom he had beaten a short head in that race. Joe describes the Brigadier's defeat at York as one of the biggest disappointments of his entire life.

'Prior to his short break after the King George, when the Guv'nor had given him a few days off, he came back none the worse for his race and everything was going to plan. Just around that time, we had the odd horse in the yard with a few symptoms – some had a temperature and a few had what we call "dirty noses" – but the Brigadier seemed normal and his work coming up to the Benson and Hedges Gold Cup was just as it had always been. I couldn't envisage any defeat whatsoever by this time, I just had so much confidence in him.'

'I don't suppose there had ever been a bigger crowd at York than on that particular day. It was packed to capacity with people who had come just to see the Brigadier. Most of my family were also there, and it was just unbelievable how I was beaten. A lot of people said that Baeza stole the race but to my mind he didn't. I thought I would be able to just go and pick him off whenever I wanted to. Sadly, I couldn't. When I pressed the accelerator, the old horse quickened up and I got to within maybe half a length and then I knew I couldn't beat him and more or less accepted it.'

It wasn't until a day later that Joe was given a clue to the defeat. 'I was talking to Buster Haslam, who has been travelling head lad for both Dick Hern and Jack Colling for about 45 years. Buster's a very sound and knowledgeable person whose word I would value more than a lot of other people's. Buster said that when the horse was being led back to the stables, he allowed the Brigadier to lower his head and a fair bit of mucus came out of his nostrils, which isn't the best of sights. I think that very possibly the old horse could have had a slight chill which could have taken the edge off him and caused his unthinkable defeat.'

John Hislop, Dick Hern and Joe Mercer still kept their faith in the horse, knowing that somewhere along the line he had just

OVERLEAF:
Two top class colts in battle. Joe on Sallust (right) gets the better of Willie Carson on the 2,000 Guineas winner High Top in an epic Sussex Stakes at Goodwood.

103

had an off day. In the Queen Elizabeth II Stakes over a mile at Ascot in late September, Hislop was adamant that the Brigadier would make amends for his defeat at York. 'John said that it would be rather nice if he could go out there and break the 15-year-old course record just to show them what he was made of. I said I thought it was a very good idea and away we went.'

Jimmy Lindley rode Almagest, the Brigadier's stable companion, who was in there to set a strong pace. Brigadier Gerard lost a few lengths as the stalls opened but it made no difference. Sparkler, receiving 7lb, who had given the Brigadier such a close race at Royal Ascot the previous year, was left standing in the final furlong as the Brigadier came clear for a six-length win. The course record had been shattered by over a second. What a comeback. 'It just showed the ability that this horse had. I only wish I could have had him for years to ride on the odd occasion!'

The Champion Stakes was to be the Brigadier's last race. As Joe says: 'It was going to be rather a sad occasion because I would be losing him. It's funny how a horse seems to sense the occasion – I swear to you that that day, the horse seemed to know that it was his last appearance on a racecourse. I could hardly hold him at the five-furlong mark and I could only hope someone would keep going. At the three-furlong pole I just had to ease him out because I was beginning to climb over the top of them. As soon as I pulled out the old horse knew it and he simply took off of his own free will – I didn't have to encourage him. The applause and noise was unbelievable as I eased him down at the finish. I've never heard such a fantastic ovation for a horse and he seemed to know, too. He stood there, a picture of equine splendour, a most magnificent beast. It was a very sad moment for me and everybody connected with him because this was his farewell to the British racing scene. I had tears in my eyes and I know other people did. It was the end of a wonderful partnership.'

The End of an Era

By the mid-1970s, 'Smokin' Joe' Mercer (he is rarely without his pipe) had passed the stage of being one of the more experienced men of the weighing-room and had become one of the seniors. Not that one would have known it from the weighing-room, where all jockeys work together so that age never comes into it. The faces change but the atmosphere remains just as friendly and, as always, provides a stage for any would-be comedian.

'Everyone's a character in their own right,' Joe reveals, 'and there are several in there that could earn a living on the stage, particularly Peter Gunn who is always full of jokes and tells them exceptionally well. A lot of people take the mickey out of Lester, but when Brian Taylor teased him, Lester would really enjoy it. "BT" did a superb imitation of him which used to make Lester double up.

'Brian and Geoff Lewis were the best golfers in the weighing-room – both had single-figure handicaps. Geoff played a lot of golf with Ronnie Corbett and Jimmy Tarbuck and obviously has a good fund of jokes. When he gets going, you can't get a word in edgeways. Once he started telling me a story in the weighing-room, it was still going when we were loaded into the stalls and he only finished the tale after about five furlongs. Of course, once Willie Carson gets the floor, there's no stopping him. If he starts laughing, then everybody starts – he has that infectious giggle.

'When Greville Starkey is busy during the season, he keeps himself to himself. But once off duty, the things he does are unbelievable. I remember one occasion when we were walking back after a lunch in the West End. We were passing a tall building surrounded by scaffolding when Greville turned to us and said "Right, watch this." He looked up at the scaffolding and yelled: "Don't do it, it's not worth it. Don't do it!" Before we knew it, some 30 people gathered round, looking up at the scaffolding and wondering what was going on. Greville beckoned us to move along and we left a crowd of puzzled people looking up behind us.

'Greville is a very kind person. He used to smuggle out pork pies and cakes for the old people that lived in the cottages near his home. But the fun went out of it when the boys in the tea rooms caught on and began to ask Greville what his requirements would be that day.

'Lester has a smashing sense of humour as well, you know. We were all out in South Africa once and were relaxing by the pool on our day off. Lester's wife, Susan, had just had her hair done and came round to join us. Lester leaned across to Tony Murray and myself and whispered, "Throw her in!" So Tony and I did the business and we all fell in the pool together. Susan took it all in good part – until she got out of the pool. She walked across to Lester, who was killing himself laughing and, looking daggers at him, dragged him off like a naughty boy!'

Joe recalls another incident that took place longer ago, in Penang one Christmas, and which led to a car chase. 'Lester had had one or two too many and took it upon himself to serve the turkey at the jockeys' dinner. He sent it flying off in different directions, taking pot luck as to whether it would land on a plate. This greatly annoyed the Australian boys and the next thing we knew we were running for our lives! We jumped into a car with me driving and Lester looking anxiously behind. Unfortunately, I took the bumper off another car as I pulled out and the chase began. We ended up parking the car down a side street and making a dash for the nearest door!'

In the '50s and '60s, Australian jockeys became regular visitors to the British racing scene. 'Bill Williamson didn't say a lot but he had a dry, witty sense of humour. I remember once when Jimmy Lindley, Bill and myself were in a restaurant and pheasant was on the menu. Jimmy went on for several minutes about how pheasant are raised, the costs of the shoot etc. and a deadpan Bill just looked at him and said, "Fine, but I don't like pheasant".

'Scobie Breasley was the same – very quiet and very precise in what he said and did. Years ago, a few of us went to Scandinavia where they race on dirt. The weather was awful – it was pouring down all day and Scobie was booked to ride in seven of the races, it being their Guineas day. Coming back into the weighing-room, you were covered from head to foot in mud. After the Guineas, Scobie had had enough of this. He said he wouldn't ride any more and promptly walked – fully clothed – into the shower! Joe Sime, the top Northern jockey, who had played a major part in drinking the 'plane dry on the way over, actually won the big race without changing his hands, because he felt so bad.'

OPPOSITE PAGE:
Now firmly established as a senior rider, Joe discusses the morning's work.

'We are all great friends, and naturally there are a lot of pranks while you're standing around half-naked in the weighing-room with the usual jokes made about the anatomy that's on display. Bob Weaver bears the brunt of a lot of these – he'd carry top weight in any handicap!'

The atmosphere in the weighing-rooms of the North differed little. As Joe says, 'A game of cards in any weighing-room is the same, no matter where it is.' 'Weighing-room rummy' was, and still is, the game and Mercer was one of its best exponents. In all the years he played, he never had a losing year. But, as he says, he'd played a lot longer than most, having first shuffled a pack of cards at the age of 12. 'When I was taught to play by the valets, the stakes were a ha'penny a point. Later, I saw games with five pounds as a stake, but the same crowd play and so the money tends to go round in circles so that nobody makes a heavy loss or gain. However, I do remember at Doncaster one day, some of the boys had started a game of poker. I wasn't impressed with the standard and as I had rides in the first and last races, I decided to play in the interim. Well, I won a bundle!'

Nobody cheated at cards in the weighing-room but several of the jockeys held jokers up their sleeves to beat the clerk of the scales. 'When I was young I used to cheat and leave the girths off. You'd take anything off you possibly could and put it back on afterwards. When the crash helmets first came in, some of us used to have bowler hats with the rims cut off so that all we had to do was to put the colours of the crash helmet on them.'

'The trouble is that the clerks of the scales know when you're doing your rock bottom weight-wise and know people that are taking advantage of them. On the other hand, there was one incident at Yarmouth a few years ago on a very wet day. I weighed out and was doing a light weight and the clerk asked both Eric Eldin and I – the two of us being quite senior at the time – to put our boots and macs on. It was throwing it down and everybody was going to be three or four pounds heavier anyway!'

As in any occupation, there are arguments with colleagues. Joe even had a rift with Jimmy Lindley once. 'We were driving to Nottingham together and were discussing the card. I told Jim that I thought mine was a good thing in the third race and had told my friends to have a bet on it. Jimmy didn't say a word. I found out why after I'd finished second – to Jimmy's mount! They had had a right touch and I was really annoyed. For a week or two we hardly spoke.'

Earlier in his career, Joe nearly had a punch-up with the irrepressible Charlie Smirke. 'One day at Windsor, he accused

110

me of having done something to him in the race. I told him to think again. He then said he'd kill me and a heated argument developed. I was all set to thump him one because, on that particular day, I would have had to hit him only once: he was on dieting pills at the time and was so light that I could have blown on him and he'd have fallen over. Mind you, if it had been the next day, when he would have been back to his normal weight, I'd have run a mile! Luckily, someone intervened and told me to forget it.'

Any arguments that develop are soon patched up with a few drinks. Besides, a jockey in a race needs more friends than enemies. 'There have been times when one of us has been in trouble in a race and the other lads have sensed the dangerous situation and have done something to prevent a nasty incident. Trouble will always be avoided where possible. I've seen jockeys ruin a winning chance by taking avoiding action.'

After the tremendous success of 1972, it was perhaps inevitable that things would quieten down a little the following year. Both Brigadier Gerard and Sallust had been retired to stud but Sun Prince was still around. He hadn't run again after winning the St James's Palace Stakes as a three-year-old and the reason he was hanging badly in his work was due to a hairline fracture of his off-fore. But he returned to Royal Ascot to land the Queen Anne Stakes, and it was the third year in succession that he had won at the Royal meeting.

1973 was also the year that Boldboy emerged as a star. The Lady Beaverbrook-owned gelding was to become very popular with the racing public. 'He was a sod as a two-year-old', recalls Joe. 'On his second outing, he dumped me three times between the paddock and the start. He had no intention of going into the stalls and he didn't.' Dick Hern then told Lady Beaverbrook, 'He'll either be a very good horse or he'll be nothing. I want to castrate him.' The owner wasn't too keen on this idea at the time and so for the next three or four weeks the trainer worked determinedly with Boldboy and took him to the stalls every single day, where Brian Proctor used to sit on him for 15 minutes. Dick Hern had to be very hard on the horse so that he would consent to enter the stalls and by the time of the Middle Park Stakes Boldboy was very tired. Brian Proctor rode him in the race, and he made the running until the last 100 yards or so and then faded to finish fourth. After all the hard training he had been through, it was a tremendous effort.

It was decided over the winter that he would be too difficult to train if left alone and so Boldboy suffered the unkindest cut of all.

111

Sharp Edge as a two-year-old. He was to win the Irish 2,000 Guineas the following spring.

From then on he proved himself a top class sprinter and miler and among his wins with Joe on his back were the Greenham Stakes at Newbury, the Diadem Stakes at Ascot and the Challenge Stakes at Newmarket in 1973, followed by the Abernant and Lockinge Stakes in 1974. Boldboy won five races in 1977 under Willie Carson after Joe had left West Ilsley.

In the spring of 1973, West Ilsley experienced further Classic glory when Sharp Edge won the Irish 2,000 Guineas for Jakie Astor. Joe remembers the steel grey as being a bit 'shoulderish' as

112

a two-year-old. 'He never shone on the grass gallops, but worked like a champion on sawdust. It was difficult to keep him sound and Dick did a marvellous job with him. After he had won comfortably enough at the Curragh, the choice was to run him in either the French Derby or the nine-furlong Prix Jean Prat, also at Chantilly. We decided on the latter and he bolted in.'

The Dick Hern stable were hopeful that Buoy, a son of Aureole, would complete the Classic double at the Curragh in the Irish Sweeps Derby. Buoy was owned by stockbroker Dick Hollingsworth, whose notable winners were all descendants of the mare Felucca – Buoy was a great grandson of hers. As Joe says, 'All these horses of Dick Hollingsworth's were big horses, 16.1 or 16.2 hands, and did virtually nothing as two-year-olds. They were damned good stayers.' Buoy neatly fits this description. He didn't run as a two-year-old and prior to his Irish Derby run he had won a maiden at Newmarket and the Predominate Stakes at Goodwood. He ran third to Weavers' Hall at the Curragh, won the Great Voltigeur Stakes at York and then finished runner up in Peleid's St Leger. 'He was a good horse,' says his jockey, 'but he just lacked a bit of pace.'

It was surprising then that at four years old the only staying race Buoy ran in was the Yorkshire Cup, which he won. His most important victory, however, was gained in the Coronation Cup at Epsom where Joe stole the race. 'I set off to make the running but at a slow pace so that nobody wanted to go on. With about seven furlongs remaining, I decided to go for home and seemed to catch everybody napping. I had ten-length advantage entering the straight and got home by a length from Tennyson with Dahlia third.'

Dahlia got her revenge in the King George VI and Queen Elizabeth Diamond Stakes when she won the race for the second successive year. Buoy was fourth, but Joe wasn't riding him. He was on the runner-up, the Queen's Highclere. 'Highclere was a very lanky filly and rather immature at two years', reflects Joe. 'She had two completely different characters. In season she was dead but out of season she was really aggressive.' Highclere ran three times as a two-year-old, winning on the last occasion at Newbury. But only the most ardent of her admirers would have considered her to be geniune Classic material at that stage. As *Racehorses of 1974* said: 'That Highclere would win a Classic was not apparent from her form as a two-year-old.'

Early in her three-year-old career, Highclere was a little disappointing in her work and wasn't impressing anybody. Joe remembers that she had 'a very big, high action which never

The first of two Classic victories for the Queen. Highclere just holds on from Polygamy in the 1,000 Guineas at Newmarket.

really got her anywhere'. Highclere, like Brigadier Gerard, was also by Queen's Hussar who had been owned by Lord Caernarvon, the father of Lord Porchester, the Queen's racing manager. Joe had ridden Queen's Hussar once as a three-year-old and had suggested to his owner that blinkers would bring about some improvement. Unfortunately for Joe, Queen's Hussar's regular partner was Scobie Breasley and the pair won their next five races together!

The next step of course was to fit Queen's Hussar's daughter with blinkers. 'She worked fantastically well. She worked twice in the blinds before the 1,000 Guineas and wore them in the race itself. They made her concentrate and she was spot on on the day.' Like Brigadier Gerard, Highclere ran in her Classic without having a warm-up race. It had been a magnificent training feat of Dick Hern's for the Brigadier to have won the 2,000 Guineas in 1971 first time out. He was to repeat that success again here with another offspring of Queen's Hussar, and it must be a coincidence that the only two Classic winning offspring of that stallion were trained by Dick Hern and ridden by Joe Mercer.

Joe gave the 12–1 chance Highclere a magnificent ride and got first run on Pat Eddery on the favourite Polygamy, trained by Peter Walwyn. But in the final furlong Polygamy had got back on terms and a tremendous battle ensued with the pair crossing the line together. Joe, however, had made it by a short head. In Claude Duval's early biography of Pat Eddery, the young jockey is quoted as saying he was 'bloody certain I had beaten Joe Mercer on the Queen's Highclere. It really was a killer when they announced the result the other way round. I couldn't believe it until I actually saw the photograph.' The Queen had therefore won her second Classic, to add to Pall Mall's win in the 1958 2,000 Guineas.

After the 1,000 Guineas, there was a big discussion concerning Highclere's next race. Joe was sure that Epsom wouldn't suit Highclere and finally it was decided to send the filly to Chantilly for the Prix de Diane, the French Oaks, which is a furlong and a half shorter than the Epsom equivalent. Joe recalls that Highclere was on her best behaviour that day at Chantilly. 'She must have been told she was owned by the Queen! In the race we travelled so easily. I gave her a crack with about one and a half to run and off she went.' Highclere beat Comtesse de Loir two lengths to become the first filly to win the English Guineas and French Oaks. Joe says 'Winning the Prix de Diane for the Queen on Highclere gave me a greater thrill than any other of my winners. There were so many patting her on the backside on the way back to the winners' enclosure that it was a wonder she didn't kick out and kill the lot of them. We were lucky in that in all her races, the cycle was right – we caught her out of season each time.'

As the successful team were flying back to England the pilot told them that he had just received a message over the radio. Neither Dick Hern nor Joe believed it when they were told that they had been invited to dine with the Royal Family at Windsor that evening. Once they had been convinced that it was really true, they decided they had had enough wine on the 'plane and wondered whether they were properly dressed for the occasion. The 'plane was diverted to Heathrow Airport and touched down

*Bustino beats Snow Knight
(left, Brian Taylor) again in
the Lingfield Derby trial.
Unfortunately the positions
were reversed at Epsom.*

in the pouring rain. A car then took Dick and Sheilah Hern and Joe and Anne Mercer to Windsor Castle where the Queen, umbrella in hand, greeted her team of 'warriors', as she called them, on the doorstep. 'The whole of the Royal Family were there and we had a wonderful evening', says Joe.

Highclere distinguished herself further with her fine second to Dahlia in the King George at Ascot but trained off after that and ended her racing career being well beaten in the Arc. Joe adds, 'I do believe that all good fillies have something masculine about them. They're not soppy, they're tough. Highclere was an example and later Time Charter was another'.

In his 14 years with Dick Hern, there was only one season in which Joe rode fewer winners than in 1974. His total of 70 was just two better than in 1968 when the virus in the stable was at its height. Yet 1974 was the year of three Classic wins. Highclere provided two of them, and Bustino the other. Bustino was owned by Lady Beaverbrook, who has always named her horses with seven letters for luck. Petoski, Niniski and Boldboy are other examples. A backward two-year-old, Bustino ran only once when third in the Acomb Stakes at York. The following spring, Bustino wasn't really pleasing in his work and was running rather free. Joe took over and rode him differently, dropping him out at the back in his work, and he began to improve.

As a maiden and in receipt of 5lb, Bustino beat Snow Knight half a length in the Sandown Classic trial and then increased that advantage by another two lengths when beating Snow Knight into third in the Ladbroke Derby trial at Lingfield. And yet Bustino could only finish fourth to Snow Knight in the Derby itself, though he hardly got the best of runs. Joe explains. 'I saw Brian Taylor up there in front on Snow Knight and thought "I'm too far back". But I was stuck and couldn't get out. All of a sudden the tempo quickened and I didn't get a clear run until far too late. We came from nowhere and were flying at the finish. Bustino proved afterwards to be an out-and-out stayer and I should have been up there from the box. I should certainly have finished a lot closer but whether I would have won is another matter.'

After being beaten only by Sagaro in the Grand Prix de Paris, Bustino came back and beat the Irish Sweeps Derby winner English Prince in the Great Voltigeur Stakes at York. Bustino then started at 11–10 favourite for the St Leger. 'We decided to have a pacemaker in the Leger. Riboson, ridden by Jimmy Lindley, was a very good horse which might even have won the race itself if he had been allowed to run on his own merit. Jimmy

118

put on a great performance and set just the right pace. I was upsides three and a half furlongs out and he looked across and said "F... off" – so I did.' Bustino ran on strongly to beat Giacometti three lengths and Riboson himself got third place. Lady Beaverbrook was clearly delighted.

Over the winter Bustino strengthened up and with some improvement in form to match his physical development, he was clearly going to take a lot of beating in any company. On his reappearance, with the help of Riboson again Bustino set a new course record over Epsom's mile and a half in beating Ashmore in the Coronation Cup to record another remarkable training feat of Dick Hern's. The track record still stands and it is rather ironic that nobody has gone round the Derby course and distance faster than Joe and yet he never actually won the big race itself.

What happened next in Bustino's career is of course already part of the folklore of Flat racing. Nobody will every forget the battle that took place between Grundy and Bustino in the King George VI and Queen Elizabeth Diamond Stakes at Ascot on 26 July 1975. The Dick Hern stable knew that Grundy, who had already won the Epsom and Irish Derby that year, had a fine turn of foot and they were determined to set a pace strong enough to sap the three-year-old's speed. Both five-year-old Kinglet and three-year-old Highest were chosen to be the pacemakers. Unfortunately Riboson was out of the reckoning as he had cracked a cannon bone on the home gallops.

For tension, excitement and emotion the race will never be matched and when anybody thinks of referring to a horse as 'running its heart out', they should think of this race first before saying anything. As soon as the stalls opened, Bustino was out and Joe had to restrain him to allow the pacemakers to go on. Frankie Durr on Highest soon took up the pace followed by Eric Eldin on Kinglet who had to take over after only five furlongs. The pace was unbelievable and in next to no time Peter O'Sullevan, commentating on television, was saying '... and they've passed the seven furlong pole already!'

Kinglet was coming to the end of his tether and Bustino was travelling so well that Joe decided to go on with half a mile still to run. Joe said later that the outcome may have been different if Riboson had been able to lead him further. This manoeuvre left Grundy flat-footed, and seeing the lead quickly established by Bustino, Pat Eddery hurriedly got to work on his mount. Turning into the straight Joe was seen at his brilliant best on Bustino, riding his mount flat out with rhythmic driving of hands and heels. Grundy was the only one able to give him chase and the

119

lead of two to three lengths began to close as the chestnut responded to Pat Eddery's whip and edged closer with each stride.

Grundy was almost upsides at the furlong marker and in a few yards he was ahead. But Joe, still riding at his very strongest though never at any stage resorting to the whip, encouraged a final effort from Bustino and to the disbelief of the crowd and Peter O'Sullevan, the four-year-old fought back. It was a ding-dong battle, until with just under half a furlong remaining, Bustino's effort faltered and Joe dropped his hands. Grundy had won the duel by half a length. The course record had been smashed by almost two and a half seconds and even Dahlia, who was five lengths back in third, had also beaten the old record.

Afterwards, Joe said: 'There cannot be a horse alive who could give Grundy a stone and hope to live with him. The pace was red hot and my horse just faltered in the last 100 yards. It was fantastic. He was so brave. He broke the track record giving away a stone. He ran a hell of a race. We gave the people something they'll never forget. It can't be bad, can it?' Lady Beaverbrook said: 'Bustino sorely missed Riboson and with the extra 14lb on his back and Joe Mercer, not using his whip because he knew Bustino was giving his all, filled me with pride as well as heartache.'

These comments were made in the heat of the moment. Eleven years later, Joe has the benefit of hindsight. He says now: 'Bustino wasn't beaten by Grundy because Grundy was the better horse. I don't care what anybody says, Bustino got beaten because he broke down half a furlong from home. He only cantered once after that. His tendon had gone and that was it. If you watch the race, he's winning, winning, winning. Then all of a sudden he changes his legs, his tongue comes out and he rolls to one side. At the time, yes, I thought we'd been beaten by the better horse, but make no mistake, Grundy was a hell of a racehorse.'

1975 was the last year that the older horses were required to give away 14lb to their juniors. From 1976, the weight-for-age, that is, the amount of weight a four-year-old has to give a three-year-old over a mile and a half in July, was reduced to 13lb. What would have happened, one wonders, if the amendment had been made a year earlier?

Joe pays Bustino the highest compliment by naming him, without hesitation, as the best mile-and-a-half performer he rode. That includes Brigadier Gerard. 'Brigadier Gerard was certainly the best from a mile to a mile and a quarter. But at a mile and a half – no way. He was whacked at the end of the King

OPPOSITE PAGE:
The dust flies as the Epsom course record is smashed. Bustino's tongue is over the bit as he wins the Coronation Cup.

George and didn't really stay. Bustino really got the trip. He broke track records at Epsom and Ascot in the highest class. Can you imagine what he would have done to Group Two or Group Three animals? If that horse didn't have speed, as some have been stupid enough to suggest, you can kick my a... from here to Timbuctoo!' Enough said.

Bustino was far and away the best horse trained at West Ilsley in 1975. But there were some other high class performers that helped Joe to a seasonal total of 93, his best for ten years. As well as Boldboy, there was Auction Ring, a high class two-year-old, who won the July Stakes at Newmarket the year before for Sir Michael Sobell and his business partner Sir Arnold Weinstock. 'Although he used to sweat up a bit, Auction Ring was a very bonny horse. He was very fast and as well as winning the July Stakes he was placed in the Gimcrack and Middle Park Stakes. As a three-year-old, the powers that be wanted to make him into a miler which he never was and never could be. Though he didn't get the trip, he ran respectably in the English Guineas. I didn't even go across to ride him in the Irish Guineas as I knew there wasn't much point.' This action might have caused the owners to raise an eyebrow or two, but eventually Auction Ring was brought back to sprinting and he ran third in the King's Stand Stakes before winning the King George Stakes at Goodwood.

At the other end of the scale there was the stayer Sea Anchor, owned by Dick Hollingsworth. As a three-year-old in 1975 Sea Anchor had won the King Edward VII Stakes at Royal Ascot and made the frame in both the Irish Sweeps Derby and the Great Voltigeur Stakes. But staying, he was another typical Hollingsworth horse, and it was always going to be his forte. So it proved in 1976 when Sea Anchor won the Henry II Stakes at Sandown, the Goodwood Stakes under a record 10st 0lb and the Doncaster Cup. He finished third to Sagaro and Crash Course in the Ascot Gold Cup and Dick Hollingsworth had to wait another ten years before winning that race with Longboat, ridden by Willie Carson. It was a race he had long been trying to win with one of his home breds.

Another good horse around at the time was Relkino, owned by Lady Beaverbrook. Relkino finished runner up to the Lester Piggott-ridden Empery in the 1976 Epsom Derby but those present at Epsom left talking about something else. That day, Derby Day 1976, the whole racing world rebounded in disbelief and astonishment when it was announced that Joe Mercer's long-running retainer with the West Ilsley stable, which had begun with Jack Colling in 1952 on the advice of Sir Gordon

122

Richards, was not to be renewed at the end of the season. Joe had actually been forewarned by Dick Hern the previous autumn that his contract would not be renewed, but it still hit him hard.

Before racing that day Lord Porchester had taken Joe over to the car park and read him a prepared statement which he was to issue to the press that afternoon. Joe had no option but to agree to the words. He says now: 'I knew it was coming, and I thought I had become immune to the shock until the announcement was made over the loudspeaker. I felt I had been poleaxed – it wasn't the sort of news you wanted to hear an hour or so before going to ride for the stable in the Derby.'

The decision to sack Joe Mercer and replace him with Willie Carson, eight years his junior, had been taken by Sir Michael Sobell and his son-in-law, Sir Arnold Weinstock, who had bought West Ilsley stables from Jakie Astor in 1970. Their horses had previously been trained by Sir Gordon Richards, as had Lady Beaverbrook's, which also came to West Ilsley at that time. West Ilsley, therefore, became almost a private stable though the owners and breeders that had already been installed there for a long time with Dick Hern were allowed to remain. Principally, these were the Queen, Lord Rotherwick, Dick Hollingsworth and Jakie Astor. None of them were to have any say in the running of the stable, which was entirely taken over by Sir Arnold. This was perfectly acceptable, as the Sobell–Weinstock partnership not only owned the stables, but also had far more horses than any other owner in the yard. The other owners were kept in the dark about the change of stable jockey and although they were far from happy at Joe's departure it made not the slightest difference.

The racing world is unusually sensitive about loyalty and John Oaksey in the *Sunday Telegraph* asked why the other owners hadn't done anything to fight for Joe. He answered the question himself, referring to the 'power structure at West Ilsley'. He wrote: 'Lack of consultation was only one reason for the owner's lack of resistance, and it is the other, to my mind, that puts the whole concept of a large stable controlled by one man who is not the trainer under what ought to be a highly critical microscope.

'Because, of course, the owners at West Ilsley feel at least as much loyalty to Dick Hern as they do to Joe Mercer. So, since an owner's only effective ultimate weapon is the withdrawal of his horses, they were on the horns of an impossible dilemma.'

As for the inevitable question – who made the decision to sack Joe in the first place? – the answer was more difficult to find.

OVERLEAF:
Joe in his study at Cold Ash Farm. His departure from West Ilsley caused shock waves throughout the racing world.

Little Stalker runs away with the 1985 Gimcrack Stakes at York, a race Joe had last won in 1966.

Newbury was one of many racecourses that honoured Joe Mercer and Lester Piggott in their retirement year. 'Smokin' Joe' is delighted with the addition to his pipe collection, while Lester displays a magnificent cigar box.

ABOVE:
Joe's perfectly-timed challenge on Time Charter carries him to victory in the King George from Diamond Shoal (Lester Piggott) and Sun Princess (Willie Carson).

LEFT:
Back in the limelight. Joe receives a memento of his popular win from the Queen.

OPPOSITE PAGE:
The closing stages of an unforgettable race. Grundy and Bustino fight it out in the King George to the exhilaration of the Ascot crowd.

There had been differences of opinion between Joe and the Weinstocks, but in view of Joe's ability as a jockey, the decision was impossible to understand. As John Oaksey wrote in that same article, 'In my considered opinion, often recorded long before this mix-up, he is not only the most stylish Flat race jockey I have ever seen, but also one of the most consistent, effective and above all reliable.'

Jack Logan of the *Sporting Life* was in no doubt about the reasons for the decision. Under the headline 'Why the knights of West Ilsley deserve praise' in his Friday Commentary column of that week, Logan wrote: 'Its real cause, of course, should be obvious to anyone familiar with the day-to-day running of a modern business ... Joe is 41. If that is not exactly the conventional age for admission to the jockeys' geriatric ward, it is at least knocking on the door of retirement. It was therefore the merest prudence for the stable owners to look around for a successor and, once found, to sign him up'.

This is now accepted as the reason for Joe's departure from West Ilsley at that time. Sir Arnold Weinstock was running a high-powered organisation into which he and his father-in-law, Sir Michael Sobell, had sunk a small fortune, together with the Ballymacoll Stud in Ireland, which they had bought from the executors of Miss Dorothy Paget. They were seeking some continuity to protect their investment and 32-year-old Willie Carson had just become freelance due to the death of his trainer, Bernard Van Cutsem, in 1975. Champion Jockey in both 1972 and 1973, Carson wasn't going to be on the market for long at his age and with his ability. Moreover, Willie could achieve 7st 10lb if necessary compared to Joe's 8st 4lb to 5lb and that was a major asset in any yard. So the switch went ahead at the end of the 1975 season, although the well-kept secret was not released until Derby Day the following year.

Joe had never stopped to consider his position under the new regime. He had been there so long that it had become a normal part of the procedure that he should air his views and pass judgement on the horses, without necessarily being asked to do so. Dick Hern valued his opinion as did Jakie Astor and the other owners. But it transpired that these views were not always to the liking of Simon Weinstock and his father Sir Arnold. At his age and with his experience, Joe certainly found it very hard to take orders from Simon Weinstock, who was then an undergraduate and just learning the game. Reflects Joe, 'In those days young Simon thought he knew everything and even questioned my riding one day at Newbury when I was beaten on a horse of theirs called Cupid. "Why didn't you come round?" he asked. I told him that there was enough room on the rails to drive a double decker bus through and that the horse simply wasn't good enough. I more or less said to Dick that if the boy wanted to tell me how to ride them, then he'd better ride them himself! I think that was the start of it all.'

Whatever the reasons for the dismissal, business and/or personal, Joe Mercer left Epsom after racing had finished facing the prospect of a completely different lifestyle as a freelance jockey. 'We were not a happy couple as I drove home at the end of Derby Day and I was almost too depressed to speak. Here I was, at the age of 41, having just lost a job which appeared safe for my lifetime. I had given the best 23 years of my life to the West Ilsley stable. Who was going to want me for the last ten years with so many up-and-coming lads about? These were some of the thoughts which were going through my mind and it worried me no end. However, after a drink at home and a chat with Anne, the telephone never stopped ringing with friends and well-wishers offering encouragement. It then began to look as though things were not quite so bad.'

At least the split with Dick Hern, who remained, and still remains, a close friend, ended without any bitterness. They had always got on well together and still see one another two or three times a year for dinner. In the ensuing years Joe was the first jockey that Dick turned to when Willie Carson wasn't available.

Champion Jockey

After the news of Joe's sacking, the letters began to pour in. The public take it to heart when their popular heroes are not treated with quite the respect they would wish. One of the letters that Joe received was particularly perceptive. It read as follows:

Dear Joe,
We would like you to know that we are appalled at the way you have been treated and I'm sure everyone who knows anything about racing is feeling the same way.

But don't give it another thought Joe – in two years time, you'll look back and think it was the best thing that could happen. An incident like this can start off a chain of events which nobody can foresee. With thousands of people all pro Joe over this, you can be sure that 'the best is yet to be'.

By the end of the week Joe was back on form, encouraged by the realisation that he was far from a forgotten man heading for the scrapheap. It was typical of Joe, that when asked about the sacking by Robin Gray of the *News of the World*, he replied: 'If I'd been the stable owners perhaps I'd have done the same.'

Then Ian Balding, with his powerful string at Kingsclere, supported by the studs of Paul Mellon, offered Joe Mercer a retainer for life. 'It was a magnificent gesture' says Joe. 'I thanked Ian but asked for time to think it over as I didn't want to make a hurried decision.'

Joe's 'phone rang again. This time it was Henry Cecil, the new Champion trainer for 1976, largely due to the successes of Wollow, who won the 2,000 Guineas, Sussex Stakes and Benson and Hedges Gold Cup. Wollow, who had started odds-on in Empery's Derby only to fail to get the trip, also had the Eclipse Stakes awarded to him after the disqualification of Trepan.

Henry Cecil had started training at Newmarket in 1968 on the retirement of his step-father, Captain Sir Cecil Boyd-Rochfort, for whom Joe's father-in-law Harry Carr had been stable jockey until his retirement in 1964. Henry Cecil had married Julie, the daughter of the legendary trainer Sir Noel Murless, and at the end of 1976 Sir Noel himself retired and handed over Warren Place stables to his son-in-law. Henry was under no illusions. He would be taking over one of the most famous training establishments in the country. Sir Noel had sent out 17 Classic winners from Warren Place, among them Crepello, Petite Etoile, St Paddy and Royal Palace. Cecil was without a jockey for the 1977 season and it was then that he called Joe Mercer.

'Henry told me that he had been discussing the matter with his leading owner Jim Joel, and they had decided to offer me a retainer for the following year. Without hesitation I accepted.'

There followed the four most successful years of Joe's career. He never rode under 100 winners in a season at Warren Place, beginning with 102 in 1977, followed by 115, 164 and 103 respectively. Joe would probably never have become Champion Jockey had he not gone to Henry Cecil. 'When I was riding at

Henry Cecil, the force behind the four most successful years of Joe's career.

West Ilsley' admits Joe, 'I was happy with my job, making a good living, and riding 70 to 80 winners a year. I was never very ambitious.'

Joe's family didn't move to Newmarket. He started off by living with his in-laws at the Genesis Green Stud just outside Newmarket, which is now owned and run by the Swinburn family. Then he moved into a flat in Newmarket itself and spent five days a week there. 'I had a wonderful relationship with Henry and his wife Julie', recalls Joe. 'I found Henry very easy to work with and we seemed to hit it off more or less straight away. Being the daughter of Noel Murless, Julie had been brought up with horses from childhood and loved them. As such she was invaluable to Henry and nothing escaped her when riding out every morning with the string. She was an enormous asset to the team and that, combined with her terrific personality, gave her a knack of keeping morale very high. She had a word and a quip for everyone.'

Joe had become quite set in his ways after 24 years at West Ilsley and he found he had to change to suit his new boss. So he came back early from a riding engagement in Hong Kong to give himself a full month before racing started to get to know the horses and the stable routine at Warren Place. Just after seven o'clock in the morning I would drive up to Warren Place and meet Henry in the kitchen over a cup of coffee. Henry would be there with his book in which all the horses' engagements were written and we'd have half an hour's chat about where the horses would be running and what work they would be doing on the gallops. Henry loved talking about his horses and treated them all as individuals. No two horses would necessarily get the same treatment, either in the stables or on the gallops. He paid meticulous attention to detail.

'If a horse had run badly, Henry would never analyse its performance immediately. He always preferred to let 24 hours go by and sometimes there would be no need to talk about it, as the reason would become apparent. The horse would be found to be running a temperature or be wrong in some other way.' Henry Cecil would work quite a long way in advance, which was very helpful to Joe as he could always fill in for other rides when he knew he would not be needed. After going through the running plans, Joe would walk around and have a chat with the lads. The Cecil string would pull out at about eight o'clock when most yards are on their way home.

Wollow had retired at the end of his three-year-old career and there didn't appear to be anything outstanding in the Cecil yard

Dick Hern (right) accompanies his new stable jockey Willie Carson and Dunfermline into the winners' enclosure after the 1977 St Leger.

at the beginning of 1977. Many of the Cecil two-year-olds were backward that year. Joe remembers one day when he, Frank Storey and 'Porky' Connolly were on Warren Hill working some two-year-olds that were thought to be quite promising. 'They obviously didn't please Henry,' remembers Joe, 'because he didn't look very happy when he cantered across on his hack. All he said was "I want another Wollow or a Bolkonski and I haven't got one," and then he cantered off!'

Although Henry Cecil sent out 74 winners in 1977, his best total to date, the only performers of any real consequence were

134

Royal Hive and Lucky Wednesday. Royal Hive, owned by Louis Freedman, was a very good staying filly by Royal Palace. She won four of her eight races, among them the Park Hill Stakes at Doncaster, and ran second in the Prix Vermeille and Yorkshire Oaks. But the best three-year-old filly of her generation was another daughter of Royal Palace, Dunfermline, trained by Dick Hern. Joe therefore missed out on winning the Oaks and St Leger for the Queen in her Silver Jubilee year.

Joe, meanwhile, struck up a successful partnership with Lucky Wednesday, a colt that had been trained in Ireland as a three-year-old. In Henry Cecil's care he improved as a four-year-old to win the Westbury Stakes at Sandown, the Clive Graham Stakes at Goodwood and the Prince of Wales Stakes at Royal Ascot. He was the only one to give Artaius a race in the Eclipse Stakes at Sandown but he broke down after running sixth to The Minstrel in the King George at Ascot. Joe could be forgiven if Lucky Wednesday's win in the Westbury Stakes gave him some personal satisfaction; on that occasion he got up to beat Willie Carson on Relkino, Joe's Derby mount of the previous year.

A finish with more than prize-money at stake. Joe, on Lucky Wednesday (right), beats his former mount Relkino and Willie Carson in the Westbury Stakes at Sandown.

135

The super-tough Gunner B
proves too strong for
Balmerino (Greville Starkey,
right) in the Coral Eclipse at
Sandown.

Among those behind Lucky Wednesday in the Prince of Wales at Royal Ascot had been a chestnut colt called Gunner B, trained by George Toft at Beverley. The previous year, Joe had ridden the colt to run second to the unknown 50-1 shot Trasi's Son in the Mecca-Dante Stakes at York before winning the Doonside Cup at Ayr. In 1977 Joe and Gunner B also took the Diomed Stakes at Epsom on Derby Day.

George Toft, however, was finding Gunner B increasingly difficult to train as he showed signs of temperant on the gallops and he had become totally unruly, often refusing to move until the long toms appeared. His owner, Mr Barrett, decided the horse needed a change of scenery and, as Joe had been so successful on him, he asked Henry Cecil to take him. When Gunner B arrived at Warren Place, he didn't leave his tantrums behind in Yorkshire. Cecil's head lad, Paddy Rudkin, decided to ride him out every morning to try to get him into shape, but the horse refused to move when reaching the start of the gallop. The only way he could be persuaded to canter was for Jimmy White, the retired travelling head lad to Noel Murless, to stand behind him and generally create a commotion. In his book *On the Level* Cecil describes Gunner B as 'tough as old boots' and as having 'more character than almost all our horses put together'.

But Gunner B, at the age of five, thrived in his new surroundings and became the outstanding older horse at Warren Place. As with Lucky Wednesday, Henry Cecil brought about improvement from a horse that appeared to have fully exposed form. Gunner B won his first four races: the Earl of Sefton Stakes at Newmarket; the Brigadier Gerard Stakes at Sandown; the Prince of Wales Stakes at Royal Ascot and the Coral Eclipse Stakes at Sandown. He ended the season with five wins from seven starts after running second to Hawaiian Sound in the Benson and Hedges Gold Cup at York and then third to Swiss Maid and Hawaiian Sound again in the Champion Stakes. Little wonder, then, that *Racehorses of 1978* described Gunner B's standard of performance as reaching new heights. What a turn-up for Henry Cecil, and all because Joe Mercer had teamed up with the colt at an earlier stage!

The real strength of the stable that season, however, lay in the potential of its two-year-olds. Near the top of the Free Handicap, headed by Bruce Hobbs's Tromos on 9st 7lb, Cecil had Formulate (9st 1lb), Lyphard's Wish and R. B. Chesne (8st 13lb); Kris (8st 12lb) and One in a Million (8st 11lb) who were both unbeaten; Odeon (8st 9lb) and Main Reef (8st 8lb). Formulate, who was to disappoint as a three-year-old, was the leading staying two-year-old filly of 1978, when she won the Waterford Candelabra Stakes at Goodwood (at 20–1 ridden by the Australian jockey Malcolm Johnson as Joe was on the stable's other runner Mixed Applause), the May Hill Stakes at Doncaster and the Hoover Fillies' Mile at Ascot.

Joe was particularly keen on R. B. Chesne, who was owned by Charles St George and was a son of Brigadier Gerard out of Vaguely Noble's sister Vive la Reine. He says 'R. B. Chesne was a very good two-year-old who won his first three starts, including the Laurent Perrier Champagne Stakes at Doncaster. He went wrong in the Middle Park Stakes and then had a lung infection the following spring. He didn't run again until September when he came second to Tap On Wood at Doncaster. I think he would have been a very good horse and was one of the very few that actually looked like his sire Brigadier Gerard.' Brigadier Gerard's great rival, Mill Reef, also had a good two-year-old in the stable in the chestnut form of Main Reef. Main Reef was a very fast two-year-old who broke the Newmarket course record under one of Joe's strongest finishes, in the July Stakes. He was to stay in training at Warren Place until 1981 and won more good races without quite reaching the top class.

Brigadier Gerard's son R B Chesne holds on from the fast-finishing More Light (Willie Carson) in the Laurent Perrier Champagne Stakes at Doncaster. He was never the same horse again.

In July 1978 the Daniel Wildenstein horses arrived at Warren Place after leaving Peter Walwyn's stable at Seven Barrows in Lambourn, following a disagreement between Walwyn and Wildenstein over Buckskin. Buckskin, a five-year-old owned by Paris art dealer Wildenstein, was considered to be the best stayer in Europe and started a short-priced favourite for the Ascot Gold Cup having already won the Prix du Cadran at Longchamp. But he could only finish fourth to Shangamuzo, ridden by Greville Starkey, who beat the Cecil-Mercer filly Royal Hive. Whatever the reason for Buckskin's failure, Daniel Wildenstein had no doubts and in a famous outburst in the unsaddling enclosure he accused Pat Eddery of, basically, not being man enough to win on Buckskin. To his great credit and at the cost of losing all the Wildenstein horses, Peter Walwyn stood by his stable jockey and so Henry Cecil became Daniel Wildenstein's trainer in England. Over the next decade or so the volatile Frenchman, for one reason or another, was to fall out with Yves Saint-Martin, Lester Piggott and Walter Swinburn. Joe Mercer actually managed to end his riding career without having felt the lash of Monsieur Wildenstein's tongue.

'There were about 30 horses,' recalls Joe, 'and their breeding was unbelievable in some cases.' The star was undoubtedly Buckskin, of whom Henry Cecil wrote 'I am reputed to have said that Buckskin is the best horse I have ever trained. That statement may have been made in the excitement of the moment after some great victory of his, but it is not far wrong.' In *My Greatest Training Triumph* Cecil also described him as 'a top class mile-and-a-half horse who, in my opinion, could have won the King George and the Arc.'

Joe thought Buckskin 'a very good horse indeed, with a great heart. Leonardo da Vinci was another of the Wildenstein horses to come to us that year and he had a very good reputation. To give an idea of how good Buckskin was, one day I rode him across the Limekilns over a mile, leading, and Leonardo couldn't get near him! Gunner B could only get to his quarters.'

Buckskin had foot trouble when he arrived at Peter Walwyn's from France and this continued to affect him throughout his career. Henry gave him time to settle down and then he and the blacksmith planned their action for Buckskin's feet. He had dropped soles, so Henry had a special type of shoe made and a leather padding between the shoe and the foot acted as a kind of shock absorber, enabling the horse to work on the firm ground without feeling it. Buckskin also had leg problems.

From the time he arrived in July, until the Doncaster Cup in

September, Buckskin was given long, slow work and the horse was at its peak on the day of the race and won easily. He then won the Jockey Club Cup even more easily and on both occasions Shangamuzo was left trailing. Joe considers that getting Buckskin on to a racecourse at all, let alone winning those races, was one of Henry's finest training feats.

As a six-year-old, Buckskin, as usual his legs wrapped up in cotton wool and bandages, put up a brilliant performance to win the Henry II Stakes at Sandown where racegoers were treated to a superb example of Joe's rhythmic-hands-and-heels style as he pushed his mount 15 lengths clear. But Buckskin's legs were showing signs of wear and Henry Cecil told Len Thomas of the *Sporting Life* after the Sandown procession that it would be a

A heavily-bandaged Buckskin quickens clear in the Doncaster Cup. Sea Pigeon is on the rails.

miracle if he got the horse fit and sound for the Gold Cup. 'He had always had suspensory trouble in his near fore and it is getting worse,' he added.

Henry Cecil did achieve the miracle of getting Buckskin to post for the 1979 Ascot Gold Cup. The stable had another runner in the race in the lengthy shape of Le Moss, owned by Carlo d'Alessio. Cecil had to run both with the two great stayers being under different ownership. As a result of a combination of diplomacy and sentiment, Joe rode Buckskin, the 10–11 favourite, though he was of the opinion that Le Moss, a 7–4 chance with Lester Piggott up, would win. Buckskin was in the driving seat turning into the straight but Le Moss ranged upsides with two furlongs to run. Buckskin wouldn't give in as Le Moss got his head in front until Joe, riding strongly and yet as sympathetically as he could, accepted the situation inside the final furlong and dropped his hands. With Lester Piggott still driving on Le Moss, the winning distance was seven lengths but this shouldn't be taken as a reflection on their respective merits. *Racehorses of 1980*, remarked 'On Gold Cup day, there wasn't, in truth, much between them – Le Moss's winning margin flattered him considerably'.

So Henry Cecil had saddled the first two in the Ascot Gold Cup – but he was heartbroken in the unsaddling enclosure! As he

The bubble bursts for Tromos (John Lynch). Joe and Lyphard's Wish are not extended to win the Craven Stakes at Newmarket.

wrote later, it was 'the unhappiest victory of my career; sorry if that sounds slightly zany, but Le Moss's Ascot Gold Cup win that year really was a very sad occasion for... Buckskin had only been kept in training as a six-year-old with this race in mind.'

Back at the beginning of that 1979 season, Joe's chances of becoming Champion Jockey at the age of 44 were considered so bleak that 20–1 was offered. This was despite the fact that he had ridden 115 winners in 1978 to finish third in the jockey's table behind Willie Carson and Pat Eddery. Henry Cecil had saddled a best-ever 109 winners and had taken the trainers' title for the second time that year. Both Joe and Henry were to enjoy a season they would never forget in 1979.

Things had started with a bang at Newmarket's Craven Meeting. On Tuesday Lyphard's Wish beat the champion two-year-old Tromos in the Craven Stakes to earn a tilt at the 2,000 Guineas. Then, on the second day, they won the Wood Ditton Stakes for unraced three-year-olds with Welsh Chanter. On Thursday came the brilliant five-length victory of One In A Million in the Nell Gwynn Stakes. At the Newbury meeting at the weekend, the stable had three more winners: War Legend and Volcanic for Daniel Wildenstein and, most important, the victory of Kris who beat Young Generation three lengths in the Clerical Medical Greenham Stakes.

After that week, the racing press devoted most of their attention to the progress of the Cecil–Mercer partnership. It was beginning to look as though Henry Cecil would follow in the footsteps of his father-in-law Noel Murless, who had pulled off the Newmarket Guineas double with Fleet and Royal Palace back in 1967.

One In A Million, a daughter of Brigadier Gerard's rival Rarity, started evens favourite for the 1,000 Guineas after winning all three of her starts. Not since Cynara, a very fast two-year-old trained by Harry Wragg in 1960, had Joe Mercer ridden such a speedy filly. He remarks: 'I thought at the time that she was as good as the colts. Her acceleration was super. Among the work riders then was Bobby Edmondson, who had been Champion Apprentice in 1972. He got a bit heavy but still rode out and one day, after we'd worked some of our better two-year-olds, he said to Henry: "When are you going to give my filly a chance?" So she worked with them one morning and simply murdered them. She didn't run until quite late on as a two-year-old but then trotted up in the Blue Seal Stakes at Ascot and the Houghton Stakes at Newmarket. The same thing happened on her re-appearance in the Nell Gwynn.'

The brilliant One In A Million (left) has already set up a winning lead in the 1,000 Guineas. Her rivals struggle in vain to close the gap.

One In A Million's victory in the 1,000 Guineas takes little describing. Always handy, Joe pressed the button with still just over three furlongs to run and she immediately took off with an incredible burst of speed. She was getting tired towards the line but the lead she had set up had been so great that Joe was still able to afford the luxury of peeping over his left shoulder to see Abbeydale a length and a half away. 'She was damned brilliant,' reflects Joe, 'a flying machine. But unfortunately she didn't last very long because she was very tiny. When she was beaten fair and square by Buz Kashi in the Coronation Stakes, only to be

awarded the race, she was coming to the end of her tether. Her last race was in the July Cup – I'd said in the spring that she was capable of winning the race, but by the time of the race, she was over the top. She didn't really get a mile and that was shown at Ascot where I think the mile is stiffer than the one at Newmarket.'

Given the choice between Kris, the Greenham winner, and Lyphard's Wish, the Craven winner, Joe decided to ride Kris in the 2,000 Guineas. A chestnut son of Sharpen Up, Kris had won on his debut at Leicester the previous June and had then defied a

10lb penalty at Folkestone. After that, Kris pulled a muscle in his quarters and wasn't seen out again until September when he came back to win at York. He then established himself as one of the best two-year-olds with a narrow win from Hardgreen in the Horris Hill Stakes at Newbury. Says Joe: 'We thought he would win more convincingly but I restrained him. I told Henry afterwards that perhaps it would have been better if I'd let him go.' Kris showed his battling qualities that day to get back and regain the lead from Hardgreen, who had taken it up at the distance.

'Is This The 2,000 Guineas Winner?' asked the *Sporting Life* after Kris had beaten Young Generation three lengths at Newbury. Kris had looked a very good horse that day when appearing to quicken twice to win. But connections of Young Generation, that is Guy Harwood and Greville Starkey, were adamant that their colt had blown up and would reverse placings at Newmarket. They were very nearly right.

Four days before the Guineas, in his final bit of work on racecourse side, Kris rapped a joint and, in the evening, there was a little heat in his leg. This caused a lot of anxiety for Henry Cecil, so close to the colt's big race. Rumours quickly spread and Kris eased in the market. For the next three days, he was confined to light exercise rather than normal exercise as Henry was forced to be very easy on him. Fortunately, he was quite sound 48 hours before the race, and as he had done all the necessary fast work it was hoped that the setback would be of no importance.

Newmarket work-watchers had been impressed with Kris's homework. 'I remember Neville Callaghan popping out of the woods to say to me "I know what'll win the Guineas now, Joe". He had been watching our colts work after seeing Tromos' Joe recalls. In the event Tromos, the brilliant two-year-old, never raced again and Kris started 15–8 favourite for the Guineas. He looked like justifying the support as he quickened without much apparent effort to join the leaders a furlong out. But Tap On Wood, a 20–1 outsider trained by Barry Hills and ridden by Steve Cauthen in his first season over here, found the better finishing speed. Under Joe's strongest riding, Kris just couldn't quicken again and he went down by half a length, with only a short head back to Young Generation. Perhaps the training setback had taken the edge off Kris. Joe said 'I don't know what went wrong, but for the only race in his life, Kris never fired. It was just one of those things.'

Thereafter, Kris and Joe Mercer, racing in the attractive apricot colours of Lord Howard de Walden, won their remaining six races that season. As *Racehorses of 1979* reported, 'Kris dominated racing at a mile in England as no other horse has done since the days of Brigadier Gerard'. After the Guineas Young Generation went on to beat the older generation of milers in the Lockinge Stakes at Newbury before winning equally impressively in the Prix Jean Prat at Chantilly from a high class field. Kris, in the meantime, had been let down by Henry Cecil but had been kept on the boil by winning a small race at Kempton as a prep-run for the St James's Palace Stakes at Royal Ascot.

Young Generation actually started favourite to beat Kris that day. But this time he was taking on a top form colt and Kris beat him by a comfortable length and a half. Kris then won the Sussex Stakes at Goodwood by five lengths from Swiss Maid – in which Thatching, champion sprinter that year, failed to stay – and then followed up in the Waterford Crystal Mile (run at Ascot because of alterations to Goodwood), and the Queen Elizabeth II Stakes (again by an impressive five lengths) at Ascot. Henry Cecil decided to postpone a crack at the mile and a quarter Champion Stakes until the following year. But Kris had one more race, in the seven-furlong Challenge Stakes in which he quickened clear to beat the high class sprinter Absalom.

At the end of the season, Kris was established as the best miler in Europe though the French had their own champion in Irish River. Irish River had won the Poule d'Essai des Poulains (French 2,000 Guineas) among his seven Group One successes (three of

Kris accelerates clear of Thatching (blinkers) and Swiss Maid to take the Sussex Stakes at Goodwood.

which were as a two-year-old); Kris's only win at that level had come in the Sussex Stakes but only because there weren't any other Group One mile races in Britain. In France they have the Prix Jacques le Marois and the Prix du Moulin over a mile, as well as the Prix d'Ispahan over an extended nine furlongs – all with Group One status. At long, long last, something is to be done to redress the balance and in 1987 the Queen Elizabeth II Stakes will be run as a Group One race for the first time. The St James's Palace Stakes though will have to wait until 1988 before being upgraded.

Kris never raced against Irish River, but his stablemate Lyphard's Wish did, going down by half a length in the Prix du Moulin de Longchamp. The proximity of Lyphard's Wish suggests that Kris would probably have beaten Irish River. That was just one of several top class efforts by Lyphard's Wish in 1979. 'He was a cheeky little horse,' reports Joe, 'and though not difficult, he'd have you off if you weren't careful! I don't think I ever rode him from behind – he liked to go from the box.'

After finishing fifth to Tap On Wood in the Guineas, in which he was ridden by Yves Saint-Martin, Lyphard's Wish won the Mecca-Dante Stakes at York before running fifth to Troy in the Derby. Lyphard's Wish was still in front at Epsom with two and a half furlongs to run but after that he got nowhere as his stamina ran out. Troy forged clear to win for Dick Hern and Willie Carson and the same combination was to do it again a year later with Henbit. Joe therefore missed out on two Derby winners as a result of his move from West Ilsley to Warren Place. But he doesn't look at it that way. 'All right, Dick had two Derby winners. But it doesn't necessarily mean that I would have ridden two Derby winners. It isn't the right way of looking at it,' he says, and there it rests.

Lyphard's Wish had started the 1979 season racing in the colours of Carlo d'Alessio, the Italian lawyer, who had enjoyed two wins in the 2,000 Guineas with Bolkonski and Wollow. Halfway through the season Lyphard's Wish was sold to Daniel Wildenstein but d'Alessio's colours were still carried with great distinction by Le Moss, who established himself as one of the greatest stayers seen since the Second World War.

As a three-year-old – he had shown promise on his only run in 1977 – Le Moss, a full brother to the 1969 Ascot Gold Cup and Arc winner Levmoss, showed himself well suited by a thorough test of stamina, winning the Queen's Vase at Royal Ascot and the March Stakes at Goodwood. He came to the St Leger unbeaten in four starts that year, but his temperament cost him the Classic.

Joe explains: 'Le Moss became very "colty" down at the start. There was a long delay as a result of the French colt Easter King becoming tangled up in the stalls and having to be destroyed. Le Moss took no interest in the race whatsoever. Turning into the straight he was in the mid-division when he received an almighty bang from another horse. All of a sudden he changed his legs and took off and we managed to get up for second behind Julio Mariner.'

After that emotional day when Le Moss beat Buckskin in the Gold Cup, the chestnut with the three white socks was ridden in all his races by Joe. With Buckskin's retirement after the Gold Cup, Le Moss took the Goodwood and Doncaster Cups to become the first horse to complete the Cup treble since Souepi in 1953. And Souepi had only dead-heated in the Doncaster Cup – with the Joe Mercer-ridden Nick La Rocca! On this occasion, with about seven furlongs to run, Joe dropped his whip. He called out to John Higgins, who was riding Henry Cecil's other runner, Francesco, 'Come on, John, give me a hand!' So Higgins closed his mount up alongside Joe's, handed over his stick and off they went. Le Moss was probably over the top when only fifth to Nicholas Bill in the Jockey Club Cup on his final start of 1979.

Henry Cecil's team was so strong that year that there is insufficient space to mention all the good horses though Tahitian King and Volcanic, both owned by Daniel Wildenstein, won good races. The filly Connaught Bridge also had a fine season.

Another big race win for Connaught Bridge in the Twickenham Stakes at Kempton Park.

149

She didn't come to herself until quite late on and missed the Oaks. She then went on to prove the best middle distance filly of the year, winning the Nassau Stakes at Goodwood, Yorkshire Oaks at York and Twickenham Stakes at Kempton. Henry Cecil also saddled Odeon, the runner-up in the Nassau.

As the season progressed into late summer, the Cecil–Mercer team were almost unbeatable and Joe found himself sitting on top of the jockey's table ahead of Willie Carson and Pat Eddery. Could he hold on to the end? Joe was also riding many winners for both Jeremy Hindley and John Sutcliffe at this time. He says: 'I used to fill in for Jeremy when I couldn't ride for Henry. He had some nice horses and didn't have a first jockey and it worked out very well. He Loves Me, Vincent, Bridestones and Rollahead are the ones that spring to mind. I won a decent race on Rollahead but I didn't like him and told the owners to get rid of him as I thought he was a goat. He was a kinky horse and you never felt safe on him even when going to post. So they got out of him, and, as it proved, he became disappointing.

'I'd ridden for John Sutcliffe for a long time. I won the 1979 Victoria Cup for him on The Adrianstan – a right old so and so. He'd either go or he wouldn't and he took no interest to halfway on that occasion, either. I think I upset one of the biggest gambles of recent years when I won the Britannia Handicap at Royal Ascot on Welsh Chanter – another grand horse of Henry's, owned by Jim Joel. John's Tender Heart finished second, having been laid out for the race. I wasn't popular with John that day, I can tell you. "You didn't offer me enough!" I joked, but he was in no mood for laughing!'

The following year Joe himself rode Tender Heart when a spectacular gamble was landed in the Royal Hunt Cup to provide more than adequate compensation for the Sutcliffe stable. Tender Heart was later expected to win the Cambridgeshire but had a diabolical run and could finish only fifth.

Towards the end of 1979, virtually anything Joe was riding was winning as the racing world rallied round to offer him mounts. The press were demanding more and more interviews with the champion elect. One particularly complimentary article by Michael Seely appeared in *The Field* under the sub-heading 'A champion among jockeys regardless of the title'. But even Joe must have had his doubts when some of Cecil's horses began coughing with a month left to go. Even when he was almost beyond reach, Joe, no doubt remembering 1967, remained cautious to the last: 'I won't believe I am Champion until I am ten in front with nine races to go' he said.

150

In the end Joe had ridden 164 winners from 608 mounts, giving him an exceptional percentage of 26·97 against Willie Carson's 142 winner from 820 rides. Willie's weight advantage had enabled him to have 212 more rides than Joe, yet he rode 22 fewer winners. No jockey had previously had to wait until he was 45 to win the title for the first time and only Sir Gordon Richards and Scobie Breasley had won it at all beyond that advanced age.

This important landmark in the career of a man who had sprung to fame when riding his first Classic winner at the age of 18 was considered sufficient justification for a celebration which was given and organised by Wilfred Sherman. Wilfred, a retired bookmaker, racehorse owner and organiser of the Stable Lads' Welfare Trust, laid on a sumptuous dinner before Christmas at the Ritz Hotel, London, at which many of racing's hierarchy mixed with Joe's friends who had helped him to the top. Joe was also a guest for dinner at 10 Downing Street with Margaret Thatcher.

It is difficult to believe that it was only eight years ago in 1979 that Henry Cecil set a new record when training the winners of

Joe and bookmaker Wilfred Sherman raise some money for charity by auctioning Brigadier Gerard's shoes.

151

128 races with first prize money of £683,971. That was over £200,000 more than any trainer had won before. To show how values have escalated, in 1985 Cecil won that sum in win and place money with two horses alone, Slip Anchor and Oh So Sharp. By the end of that season the stable had won £1,148,149 in first place money with a new record of 132 races won. The brilliant mare Pebbles became the first British-trained racehorse to win over £1 million in a season that year. In 1986 Michael Stoute even topped the £2 million mark in win and place money, of which £1,269,933 was for first place.

Joe will be eternally grateful to Henry Cecil for making him Champion. 'It was really Henry that put me there. Halfway through the year he said to me, "Don't worry, I'm going to make you Champion"'. If at any time Willie Carson was in a threatening position it was always Henry who came along to give Joe confidence and to tell him that he had plenty of winners lined up for him at the minor meetings which would ensure that Joe kept the lead to the end of the season. 'He is the greatest placer of a horse I have ever known' says Joe.

Henry Cecil paid his own tribute to Joe in his book *On the Level*: 'Joe Mercer ... is a true professional and a very stylish rider who keeps his horses so perfectly balanced that they always run for him. He was retained by us the year he became Champion, 1979, and deserved to be acclaimed as a truly great one, as he was absolutely brilliant. At 45, he was by no means a young man in years, but very much one at heart and proved himself a real master of his craft.'

From Warren Place to Seven Barrows

At the beginning of the 1980 season, Joe Mercer, awarded the OBE in the New Year's Honours list, was confident of successfully defending the Champion Jockey's title. Any jockey needs a good start to the season if he is to mount a serious threat in the title race, but unfortunately Joe didn't get it. He explains: 'Henry had put himself out to make sure I won the Championship and he'd used up a lot of maidens which normally would have been kept back for the following year. As it was, because they had won, they were already handicapped – most of them harshly.'

But there was no denying the strength of the Cecil team that year. Both Kris and Le Moss were kept in training and the stable had done exceptionally well with its two-year-olds in 1979, most notably with Hello Gorgeous, Many Moons, Super Asset, Marathon Gold, Suavity and La Legende, winners of 19 races between them. There was also the promising colt Ginistrelli, unbeaten in both his starts; Evita, who had won her only race; and the unraced Daniel Wildenstein-owned filly Saison.

Like One In A Million, Evita, a filly by Reform out of a half-sister to Highest Hopes and owned by Lord Howard de Walden, followed her Blue Seal Stakes win at Ascot by taking the Nell Gwynn Stakes at Newmarket on her reappearance. As winner of both of her races, she was many people's idea of the 1,000 Guineas winner. But the Cecil stable already had the 1,000 Guineas favourite, and she hadn't even run yet! This was Saison, who had been backed for the race throughout the winter. Joe recalls: 'Her homework was brilliant and when she ran in a seven-furlong newcomers' race at Newbury, it was just a case of by how far she was going to win. She won very easily.'

In the Guineas, Joe rode Saison in preference to Evita (Pat Eddery) but both finished well beaten behind Quick As Lightning. Both fillies in fact failed to win again in Britain, though Saison later fulfilled her potential by doing very well in the United States. Two days afterwards the Cecil stable was not represented in the 2,000 Guineas. It had been hoped that Hello

153

Gorgeous would line up for the race. Daniel Wildenstein's good-looking colt had won three of his four starts as a two-year-old and had become the first horse to win both the Royal Lodge Stakes and the William Hill Futurity Stakes. But he could only manage fifth place behind Final Straw in the Greenham Stakes at Newbury, and after that his target was the Epsom Derby.

Ginistrelli, who had won the Lingfield Derby trial after running third to Henbit at Sandown was also bound for Epsom — that was until he could finish only third to Prince Bee in the Predominate Stakes at Goodwood. After that he was never seen out again. Super Asset, winner of the Horris Hill Stakes at two and the highest rated English two-year-old on the 1979 Free Handicap, didn't train on and finally Hello Gorgeous was indeed Henry Cecil's only runner in the Derby.

Joe had given Hello Gorgeous a magnificent ride to win the Mecca-Dante Stakes at York, finishing well to beat Master Willie on the line. Hello Gorgeous had been under pressure from some way out and had run on so strongly that it looked as though he would stay a mile and a half, despite being by the American sprinter, Mr Prospector. Unfortunately, at Epsom Hello Gorgeous, after going as well as anything with a quarter of a mile to run, ran out of stamina and came home sixth behind Henbit, trained by Dick Hern and ridden by Willie Carson. Master Willie was second.

On 2,000 Guineas day, Henry Cecil and Joe Mercer were up at Haydock. The reason was the reappearance of Kris in a conditions race named the Cold Shield Windows Trophy. The great miler looked in need of the race and had to battle to beat the Irish Cambridgeshire winner Habituate a length, breaking the course record for Haydock's extended seven furlongs in the process, despite jumping the shadow of the winning post. Kris then broke the Newbury mile record, his third consecutive record-breaking performance, in the Tote Lockinge Stakes. Says Joe: 'I only just scrambled home there. The runners were bunched and things were very tight. Eventually I got a gap and squeezed through to get the race. A stewards' inquiry followed and as always in those instances, Henry was pulling his hair out! I think if I had lost the race he would have shot me on the spot.'

Kris's mid-season target was the Eclipse Stakes and his next run was to be the Queen Anne Stakes at Royal Ascot. But a pulled muscle in his back and a series of other niggling problems meant that that race, along with the Sussex Stakes and Waterford Crystal Mile, took place without him. According to Henry Cecil Kris 'was never the same horse again', although you wouldn't

OPPOSITE PAGE:
Another winner in the Wildenstein colours for Joe. Hello Gorgeous takes the Royal Lodge Stakes at Ascot in 1979.

154

have known it when he finally reappeared in the Crown of Crown Stakes at Goodwood in September. The four runners in opposition weren't up to top class, but they weren't useless either. Kris completely outclassed them, quickly drawing clear under Joe's urgings to win by an easy 12 lengths. The only problems in that particular race had occurred in trying to get Kris into the stalls. Joe explains: 'Kris was getting very sticky at home and he became very moody at the stalls. It was only due to the fantastic stalls handlers that he lined up at all at Goodwood. They virtually carried him in. He had to have a stalls test at Yarmouth after that, though it seemed a bit pointless at that stage when his racing career was shortly to end anyway.

'I remember working Kris one morning. We cantered down the sand at the side of the Limekilns and at the bottom he walked across the road and stopped right in the middle. Miss Clayton, a well known figure at Newmarket, was out walking her Alsatians and she was trying to shoosh me across the road. Kris didn't flinch as the traffic began to build up on both sides. I daren't get off him in case he got loose. After what seemed an eternity, he finally walked across to the gallop.'

Kris was made 2–1 on favourite to beat Known Fact (3–1) in the Queen Elizabeth II Stakes at Ascot. Kris came to the race having won 14 of his 15 races. Known Fact, who had won the Middle Park Stakes at two, had finished second to Nureyev in the 2,000 Guineas but the winner had interfered with the eventual third, Posse, and after a lengthy stewards' inquiry had been disqualified and placed last. Known Fact, who had escaped any of the trouble had looked fortunate to have had the race awarded to him, but nonetheless he had gone on to establish himself as a top class miler with wins in the Waterford Crystal Mile at Goodwood and Kiveton Park Steel Stakes at Doncaster.

Kris was taken to the start early at Ascot. Henry Cecil describes the scene in his book *On the Level*: 'The haunting picture of him standing behind the stalls, becoming steadily black with sweat, and Joe borrowing a handkerchief from the stalls handler to wipe his sweat-soaked reins, often flashes through my mind.' But whatever the reason for this marked aversion to the stalls, Kris could not have been a more genuine racehorse and he demonstrated it again here in what many thought was the race of the year. 'Paul Kelleway's horse Star Way made the running and I tracked him,' Joe relates. 'I took it up turning into the straight and kicked for home. Kris responded very well but Known Fact, receiving 7lb, came at him and just ran him out of it.' It was another tremendous duel, reminiscent of that between Grundy and Bustino, though this time Willie Carson was the jockey in opposition. With a furlong to run Known Fact just edged in front and, as hard as he tried to get back, Kris was still a neck down at the line. The rest were well beaten. After the race, both Joe and Henry Cecil felt that Kris had done enough racing and Lord Howard de Walden decided to retire him so the colt never actually raced beyond a mile.

Kris has also proved himself a champion at stud. From his first crop came Oh So Sharp which, in Henry Cecil's care, became the first filly for 30 years to complete the Triple Crown of the 1,000 Guineas, Oaks and St Leger. There was also Fitnah, one of the best fillies in France, and the top class two-year-old Reach. Kris got another Classic winner in 1986 when Flash of Steel won the Irish 2,000 Guineas while Sure Blade followed in his sire's hoofprints by winning the St James's Palace Stakes and Queen Elizabeth II Stakes. It is very rare for a sire to produce one Classic winner with his first crop and a record to produce three. Lord Howard de Walden can now name his own fee for a service to his young sire. Joe is not sure that Kris would have stayed a mile and a quarter. 'He used to take quite a pull. He was as good a miler as I sat on and that includes Brigadier Gerard. Kris was brilliant at both seven furlongs and a mile. He had a super turn of foot – always the hallmark of a good horse. But I wouldn't have thought he'd have been quite as good at six furlongs. I think Brigadier Gerard, on the other hand, could have won a six-furlong race.'

While Kris's 1980 campaign was slightly anti-climactic, Le Moss enjoyed his best season, though it was touch and go whether he'd be ready in time to run in the Ascot Gold Cup. In the spring of 1980 Le Moss was confined to his box for six weeks after pulling a muscle. After he had recovered from that, the problem for Henry Cecil was to get Le Moss race fit. By this time though, Le Moss had become very surly at home and refused point blank to go on any gallop. There was only one man in the yard for whom Le Moss would go and that was Alan Welbourne. Alan and Le Moss used to go off on their own, rather than work with the main string. As Henry Cecil relates in *My Greatest Training Triumph*: 'Le Moss seemed to enjoy this preferential treatment and strutted around the Heath, but with Alan weighing about ten and a half stone, the old horse was doing a little bit more than he thought.' In the evenings Cecil sent Le Moss to the equine pool for more exercise.

Come the day of the Gold Cup, Henry Cecil wasn't particularly optimistic about Le Moss's chances. 'The trouble with

OVERLEAF:
Le Moss and Ardross captured in battle in the Goodwood Cup, the second of their three epic encounters.

157

horses like this is that you always fear they're going to turn it in during a race itself, that one day they'll just not bother. Horses who simply refuse to work at home give a trainer nightmares . . .' Henry needn't have worried. As in all the Cup races that year Joe Mercer showed himself a master of judging the pace when Le Moss scored an all-the-way win over Ardross in the first of three marvellous encounters.

Joe commentates on the running of the Ascot Gold Cup: 'The French challenger Croque Monsieur took me on. He tried to get by me for a mile and a quarter but couldn't. Every time the French jockey tried to get on terms, Le Moss kept pulling out more. It was a furious pace and I thought "God, we've gone too fast!" As Croque Monsieur dropped away going to Swinley Bottom, I felt Le Moss take a breather – I could have done with one too! – and I stood up in the irons for a split second.' From the five-furlong marker both Joe and Le Moss were flat out. They seemed made for each other; the chestnut with the powerful action, emphasised by his three white socks, and the jockey, crouched low, punching and swinging the whip in perfect rhythm with the horse's action. Neither Joe nor Le Moss let up before the line, where the margin over the sole challenger Ardross was threequarters of a length. Joe, who was dead beat after the race, is in no doubt about the magnitude of Henry Cecil's training feat. 'It was one of Henry's finest achievements to get Le Moss on the track to win the Gold Cup without a preparatory race,' he says. 'Le Moss was spot on and to win the race in the style he did – well, it really was a hell of a feat.'

In both the Goodwood (two miles five furlongs) and Doncaster (two and a quarter miles) Cups Le Moss had to give 2lb to Ardross. At Goodwood, Greville Starkey on Donegal Prince gave hand signals to Christy Roche on Ardross as the Irishman had never seen the course before. As they came to each bend, Greville put out the appropriate arm! Ardross, as at Ascot, came to challenge Le Moss, flat out from the six-furlong marker, in the straight. Again, Le Moss refused to surrender the lead, and he was a neck to the good at the line. The winning distance and the running of the race was the same at Town Moor, Doncaster. It was Joe's eighth Doncaster Cup win – a record.

Le Moss had become the only horse to complete the stayers' Triple Crown two years in succession. He had done it the hard way, making all the running. He made his final appearance in the Prix Gladiateur at Longchamp. *Racehorses of 1980* reports: 'The success Le Moss enjoyed in a fine career was due in no small measure to the fine handling he received from his regular jockey

Mercer, but for once Mercer didn't ride a good race in the Gladiateur.' Le Moss went down by half a length to the filly Anifa the day after Kris had been beaten by Known Fact at Ascot. Joe agrees he didn't go fast enough. 'By now,' he says, 'the French jockeys had an idea of what sort of horse they had to beat. Le Moss always picked up when challenged, so Anifa's challenge came late and very wide. Although he was about two lengths down, Le Moss fought back and was down only half a length at the line. He'd have won it on his head had he been challenged a mile out.'

Although Anifa franked the form with a decisive win in the Turf Classic at Aqueduct it was a pity that Le Moss had ended his racing career in defeat. But the duels with Ardross will not be forgotten for a long time. As for Joe Mercer's contribution to Le Moss's success, Henry Cecil wrote, 'There's no doubt that Joe Mercer helped. He rode Le Moss magnificently: no jockey could have ridden him better and they seemed to work together in perfect rhythm. Joe was unbelievable on certain horses; Kris and Light Cavalry would be two others I'd pick out, and without taking anything away from Lester, I would far rather have had Joe on Light Cavalry in 1981 than Lester.'

Lester Piggott, of course, took over the role of stable jockey at Warren Place in 1981 when he, Pat Eddery and Joe Mercer played 'musical stables' at the end of the 1980 season. Joe takes up the story. 'Jimmy Lindley approached me in August and told me that Pat Eddery was leaving Peter Walwyn and going to ride for Robert Sangster in 1981 as a result of Sangster and Lester splitting up. This was the first I'd heard of it but Peter Walwyn had asked Jimmy to ask me if I wanted the job at Seven Barrows. I wanted time to think about it. In the meantime, the rift between Lester and Sangster had become public. I think I had to make up my mind by early September and I discussed it with Anne. She just said it was up to me. I also had a drink and a chat with Dick Hern, to ask him what he thought. He said "knowing you, the only advice I can give you is do what you think will be best for you to be happy". Well, I thought about that and came to the conclusion that I would be happiest back home.'

Joe had been clocking up a magnificent mileage since he'd been riding for Henry Cecil. 'I known it sounds trivial for somebody who's single, but driving backwards and forwards for four years when the rest of the traffic is going the other way isn't easy. I saw a lot of Henry and Sarah, my two eldest children, when they were small, but very little of Joe, the youngest. I used to come home at nights and he'd be in bed, and I would be gone

before he'd woken up in the morning. Sometimes I wouldn't see him for a week and I was like a stranger to him.

'With Lester free again, I had also heard rumours about him taking over at Henry Cecil's. I know that I certainly wouldn't have been riding the horses owned by Charles St George in 1981. I'd had the most successful spell of my career riding for Henry, but money isn't everything and so I decided to take up Peter Walwyn's offer. I just felt it would be best for me as a man of 46 years of age to be back home with a good job. I didn't get a chance to discuss it with Henry himself as he was away at the sales in the States. I finally managed to take him to one side at the Doncaster St Leger meeting. He told me he had heard the news and I wanted to explain the situation, that I had heard I would have been disappointed if I had continued to ride for him. Of course, Henry said nothing about that as there was nothing he could say, but he understood my reasons for returning to Berkshire and we parted on smashing terms. We're still great friends and if I have a chance to pop in, I always do.'

The Cecil–Mercer team had tremendous success at Doncaster that week. On Wednesday Joe gave the Charles St George-owned Gielgud a brilliant ride to win the Laurent Perrier Champagne Stakes. The following day Le Moss won the Doncaster Cup and then on Friday Joe went down to Goodwood to ride Kris in his easy comeback win after his long lay-off. The week was crowned by the success of Light Cavalry, owned by Jim Joel, in the St Leger. It isn't often you see a jockey set out to make all the running in the oldest Classic but that is exactly what Joe Mercer did. When the 11–8 favourite, Water Mill, a son of Mill Reef, looked like getting on terms with two furlongs to run, Light Cavalry found extra and came clear to win by four lengths. Light Cavalry had already won the King Edward VII Stakes at Royal Ascot and after that ran two good races in defeat, with Henry Cecil promising improvement at Doncaster. As he recounts in his own book, 'I was exuding confidence on St Leger day. Light Cavalry had worked very well, and had never been better in himself in the whole of his career.'

In winning the St Leger Light Cavalry, described by Joe as a 'lovely kind horse', also gave his sire Brigadier Gerard his first Classic winner. How fitting that Joe should have ridden it. No wonder he had a smile on his face as he passed the finishing post. The golden autumn for Henry and Joe continued when the two-year-old filly Pushy, owned by the Marchioness of Tavistock, won the Cornwallis Stakes at Ascot to add to her Queen Mary success at Royal Ascot. The Tavistocks are good friends of Joe's

OPPOSITE PAGE:
Joe with Lester Piggott, who took over his job as stable jockey at Warren Place. 'I'll take the cheque, you take the sword'!

OVERLEAF. LEFT:
A brilliant piece of jockeyship. Light Cavalry makes all the running in the 1980 St Leger to give Joe the perfect finishing touch to his association with Henry Cecil.

RIGHT:
The St Leger cap is hardly a perfect fit, but it doesn't seem to worry Joe!

and he was delighted to ride their first Group race winner for them.

Light Cavalry's dam, Glass Slipper, made history the following spring when her daughter by Mill Reef, Fairy Footsteps, won the 1,000 Guineas to provide Jim Joel and Henry Cecil with consecutive Classic wins. The filly was ridden by the new stable jockey Lester Piggott, who was also to enjoy something of a revival with Henry Cecil. With Cecil's help Lester regained the Champion Jockey's title he had last held in 1971 and retained it in 1982. Lester also remained at Warren Place for four years until the disagreement with Daniel Wildenstein led to him going freelance again for his final season in 1985.

Before Joe took up his new position, he joined Greville Starkey, Paul Cook and Willie Carson to ride in Argentina for a week. 'We went out there for a week as an experiment. There was no money in it but it was a success and would have become a regular thing but for the Falklands War. It was a fantastic place and I found the people very friendly. The racetrack at San Isidro in Buenos Aires was beautiful. Prices seemed to go up by the

Another Group race win for the little filly Pushy in the Cornwallis Stakes at Ascot.

hour, though. You would buy a drink one day and it would be more expensive the next.'

Joe had ended the 1980 season with 103 winners, finishing fifth to Willie Carson. That year, Dick Hern regained the trainers' title last won in 1972 after a fine season which saw him win the Derby with Henbit, the Oaks with Bireme and the King George with Ela-Mana-Mou. Joe must have hoped that Peter Walwyn would also be staging a revival of those heady days of the mid-1970s when he had been Champion Trainer in both 1974 and 1975.

'The Ultimate Professional'

Peter Walwyn had taken out a licence to train at Lambourn in 1960 after assisting his cousin, Helen Johnson-Houghton. He bought Seven Barrows from the Candy family and started training there in 1965. Says Joe: 'I rode for Pete donkey's years ago when he first started; horses like Be Hopeful, who won 26 races, and Chevington. We're great pals. When he moved to Seven Barrows and his stable grew, he offered me the job of stable jockey. I was still with Dick and suggested Duncan Keith,

Joe's friend and last guv'nor, Peter Walwyn.

168

who got the job. Unfortunately Duncan had his weight problems and in 1969 Peter offered me an open cheque to ride for him again. I was flattered but I explained I was still happy riding for Dick despite all the problems we'd been having with the virus. It was then that I recommended Pat Eddery because I believed he was a brilliant young jockey. We used to call Pat "Polyfilla" because he filled any gaps in a race.'

Peter Walwyn's first big win came in the 1965 Yorkshire Oaks with Mabel – ridden by Joe Mercer! Since then he had won the 1970 1,000 Guineas with Humble Duty, 1974 Oaks with Polygamy, 1975 Derby with the great Grundy as well as other top races with the likes of Rock Roi, Habat, May Hill, Orange Bay, Vitiges, Formidable and Crow. But since 1978 the stable have had mixed fortunes due to recurring bouts of the virus. Joe adds 'Somewhere along the line Pete has also lost quite a lot of the old individual owners such as the Williams (Mabel and Be Hopeful). Then in 1978 Daniel Wildenstein took his horses away after the Buckskin disagreement. Finally, Stavros Niarchos pulled out in the year I came.'

In 1981, Joe's previous master Henry Cecil saddled 107 winners, but Joe's own total dropped from 104 in 1980 to 64. Joe had some decent outside rides, such as Norwick in the Royal Lodge Stakes for Guy Harwood, but Peter Walwyn had no outstanding horses though the very useful two-year-old filly Travel On won the Cherry Hinton Stakes at Newmarket at 25–1. It was to be the stable's only British pattern race win for four years. But the most notable win for the Walwyn–Mercer team that year was recorded by Halsbury in the Tote Cesarewitch. It was Halsbury's tenth race of the season – he had won four of the previous nine. It says much for the training skills of Peter Walwyn that a horse that was entitled to be fully exposed was still able to take this most competitive of races. After two and a quarter miles, Joe, at 47, showed the dash of a young man in helping Halsbury to keep going to the line.

It was the unfortunate accident to Willie Carson on Silken Knot in the Yorkshire Oaks in August that brought about a dramatic revival in Joe's fortunes. Turning into the straight at York, Silken Knot fell and broke both her forelegs. It was a horrific accident and looked appalling from the stands. The filly came to a halt in the most distressing manner and Willie was badly injured and out for the rest of the season. He spent a month in hospital and his full recuperation took a long time.

For the rest of the season, Lester Piggott and Joe Mercer more or less shared the Dick Hern rides. Hern had two runners in the

169

Travel On takes the Cherry Hinton Stakes for the Walwyn stable. There was to be a long wait for further success at that level.

St Leger in Lester's mount Bustomi, winner of the King Edward VII Stakes at Ascot and the Gordon Stakes at Goodwood, and Joe's ride Cut Above, runner-up to Shergar in the Irish Sweeps Derby. Shergar of course started 9–4 on for the Leger. Bustomi was third in the betting a 13–2 after Glint of Gold (4–1) and Cut Above, owned by the now Sir Jakie Astor and a half-brother to Joe's 1973 Irish Guineas winner Sharp Edge, was next at what turned out to be a very generous 28–1. These four were clear going into the straight but it was Joe who was first to get down to work. Shergar, who according to Joe, was making 'a hell of a noise', was beaten with three furlongs to run. Glint of Gold moved into the lead with two to run but Joe forced Cut Above into overdrive and the combination stayed on to beat Glint of Gold by two and a half lengths with Bustomi third and Shergar only fourth. No matter how few winners a jockey rides in a season, one Classic winner is enough to make it a good year.

170

'The old firm strike again as Shergar is vanquished' proclaimed the *Sporting Life*. Sixteen years after Provoke had won the St Leger at the same price, 28–1, for Sir Jakie Astor, Dick Hern and Joe Mercer, history had repeated itself. A memorable day for Joe was completed when the Queen's filly, Height of Fashion, won the May Hill Stakes from the Henry Cecil-trained Clare Island ridden by Lester Piggott. Height of Fashion was a daughter of Joe's old favourites Bustino and Highclere. Joe had also won the 1979 Lingfield Derby trial on another of Highclere's offspring, Milford, while Willie Carson had been under suspension. Height of Fashion then made all the running under Joe to take the Hoover Fillies' Mile at Ascot, ending her two-year-old career the winner of all three of her starts.

On the Monday after the Leger triumph, Joe partnered Sir Michael Sobell's Prince Bee to win the Valdoe Stakes at Goodwood for Dick Hern. The four-year-old was quietly fancied for

The chips are down at the end of the 1981 Cesarewitch. The blinkered Halsbury responds to some vigorous riding from Joe to beat Heighlin (Steve Jobar) and Military Band (George Duffield, centre).

OVERLEAF:
In Willie Carson's absence Joe Mercer wins the Hoover Fillies' Mile on Height of Fashion. The Queen's filly, ears pricked, beats Stratospheric (Pat Eddery, left).

the Arc where Joe rode him in preference to Cut Above (Brian Taylor) but both were well beaten behind Gold River. Over the winter Joe went out to ride in Hong Kong. He had been there for the first time in 1971–2, when racing had first turned professional, to ride in the Invitation Cup. 'I rode a couple of winners from a half a dozen mounts and liked it very much. I finished up winning the last race I rode in only to be told by the other jockeys that it was a farewell present! I don't think they were joking, either!'

Joe had a particularly successful time in Hong Kong in the 1976–77 season when he was retained by T. C. Cheng, a former jockey, in his first season as a trainer. (In December 1986 Cheng was to be banned for three years following allegations of bribery and corruption on the Hong Kong racing scene.) Otherwise, Joe used to go there principally for a holiday and was delighted to ride if asked. In January 1982 he was given the ride on Football, after Brian Taylor had been stood down, in the Hong Kong Derby. Football had won three modest races for Peter Walwyn and Joe in 1981 before being sent to Cheng. Football had only an outsider's chance in the Derby but nobody told him that, and Joe produced him with a devasting late burst to cut down Gilgit, who was considered a certainty at 5–1 on! An article in Hong Kong's racing monthly *Racing World* reported: 'By our estimation Football, in downing Gilgit in the Derby, improved approximately two stone from when the pair had last met 16 days previously in the Chinese Club Cup. A remarkable improvement – it's a wonder what blinkers and Joe Mercer can do for a horse!' They added that 'It would not be extravagant to say Joe Mercer is among the top half-dozen jockeys riding in the world today.'

Back in Britain for the 1982 season, Joe looked to have a great chance of bringing off a Derby double. With Pat Eddery committed to Vincent O'Brien's Golden Fleece, Jeremy Tree booked Joe to ride Peacetime, like Golden Fleece a son of Nijinsky, in the Epsom Derby. It was to be Joe's 29th try at the race. Peacetime had followed Troy, Henbit and Shergar when winning the Guardian Classic Trial at Sandown in the hands of Pat Eddery. After that, a bout of coughing interrupted the colt's training schedule and Joe gave him a brilliantly sympathetic ride when winning the Predominate Stakes at Goodwood.

Joe told Monty Court of the *Daily Mirror* that he wouldn't swap his mount with anybody, adding 'I promise you that Peacetime will give an exceptional account of himself. He is going to run a very good race.' Everything suggested that Peacetime, still running in the colours of Jock Whitney, who had

died in February, would do just that. He had looked big at Goodwood and had still given 8lb and a beating to Touching Wood. Joe gave Peacetime every chance at Epsom, and indeed looked like hacking up turning into the straight as nothing was travelling better. But he found absolutely nothing when asked and as Joe says 'didn't come home from the two-furlong marker'. Peacetime finished seventh to Golden Fleece and Touching Wood in the fastest Derby since 1935, and interestingly Joe thinks that the trip found his mount out. 'For me he didn't get a mile and a half in a true run race. They found Peacetime had a problem with his wind after the Derby (he had been hobdayed at two) and never really came right. It was disappointing because I really thought this was my chance.'

Peacetime on his way to the start at Goodwood. A breathing problem prevented him from realising his potential.

Joe ends a disappointing season in style. Century City humps top weight to victory in the 1982 Cambridgeshire from Steve Cauthen and Indian Trail.

Later in the month, Newmarket trainer Hugh Collingridge booked Joe to ride Buzzards Bay in the Royal Hunt Cup. Buzzards Bay had plenty of ability but only he knew whether he was in the mood to produce it. According to his trainer, 'Joe sat as quiet as a mouse and kidded him to victory'. It was Joe's second win in three years in that particular race following Tender Heart in 1980. In the autumn, Luca Cumani put Joe up on the Ivan Allan-owned Century City in the William Hill Cambridgeshire. At halfway Century City was last on the stands-side group, but from that point the big colt kept finding more and burst through to lead inside the final furlong. Joe got home by a neck on the 20–1 shot from Steve Cauthen on Indian Trail. It was Joe's first win in the Cambridgeshire, and Century City under 9st 6lb had set a weight-carrying record for a three-year-old in the race. Luca Cumani equalled the feat when saddling Dallas to win the race in 1986 under an identical weight.

But pattern race wins had been a bit thin on the ground since Joe had left Henry Cecil's. The useful handicapper Hill's Pageant won the Group Three Hessen-Pokal at Frankfurt in July 1983 for

Peter Walywn and Joe but that was the only success they were to have at that sort of level until Stalker won the 1985 Gimcrack Stakes. (Joe wasn't on the stable's Wagoner when the four-year-old was awarded the 1984 Doncaster Cup at the expense of first-past-the-post Petrizzo.) But the highlight of that month, and indeed of 1983, was Time Charter's win in the King George VI and Queen Elizabeth Diamond Stakes.

Time Charter had won the previous season's Oaks and Champion Stakes. Prior to the King George, Henry Candy's filly had finished a sympathetically-handled second to Electric in the Jockey Club Stakes but then hadn't been given a particularly enterprising ride when coming in only sixth to Solford in a slowly-run Eclipse Stakes. Time Charter's regular jockey, Billy Newnes, was injured on the gallops nine days before the King George. 'If it hadn't have been for Anne, I wouldn't have ridden her' Joe reveals. 'My year wasn't going that well and Anne suggested that I ring up. "After all," she said, "you've ridden for the family for 20-odd years." I was of the opinion that if they wanted me they would 'phone me, but eventually I gave in and rang. Henry Candy answered and said "It's about time you 'phoned!". The only time I sat on Time Charter prior to the race was in a canter and she went like a ball of fire. Billy Newnes told me exactly how to ride her. She ran a fabulous race.'

The King George field was a particularly good one. Joint favourites were the French Derby winner Caerleon and 12-lengths Oaks heroine Sun Princess, ridden by Willie Carson for Dick Hern. The others included the leading older horse in Britain, Diamond Shoal (Lester Piggott) and the Derby second Carlingford Castle. Joe waited with Time Charter until the turn into the straight when they came with a sustained challenge to catch and pass Diamond Shoal and Sun Princess and to win by threequarters of a length and a length. Joe's timing was as good as it had ever been and it was his first Group One win since Cut Above's St Leger. The performance won Joe the Amoco Jockey of the Month award. A *Sporting Life* reader, Ian Simpson, reckoned that Joe should also have won the award for the following month for his riding of Charlie Nelson's Double Schwartz in the Convivial Stakes at York's Ebor meeting. Joe, showing superb balance and patience, just got the two-year-old home in a tight finish from the favourite Tocave Botta, ridden by Walter Swinburn. Mr Simpson wrote: 'Although winning by only a short head, Mercer got home without resorting to the whip. I am sure that his kindness will pay dividends later in the horse's career.' How right he was proved to be! Double Schwartz

177

A contrast in styles. Walter Swinburn goes for everything on Tocave Botta but a perfectly-balanced Joe just has the upper hand on the sweating Double Schwartz.

may never have developed into Britain's Champion sprinter in 1986 had he been subjected to a hard race that day.

Time Charter had her regular jockey back for the rest of that season. She won the Prix Foy from All Along before lining up as favourite for the Arc. She ran another fine race to finish a close fourth to All Along, Sun Princess and Luth Enchantee. The four-year-old filly All Along, trained by Patrick-Louis Biancone, was ridden by Walter Swinburn for Daniel Wildenstein. But it could so easily have been Joe Mercer in the saddle. Joe explains: 'I was asked at Ascot the previous week if I wanted to ride All Along in the Arc. Daniel Wildenstein had expected Lester to ride her but Lester preferred the 1982 Arc third Awaasif for John Dunlop

*Happy 50th birthday, Joe!
From left: Richard Fox,
Steve Dawson, Joe, Dominic
Gibson, John Matthias,
Lester Piggott, Steve
Cauthen and Greville
Starkey.*

who subsequently finished 13th to All Along. By this time I had agreed to ride Sailor's Dance for Dick as a pacemaker for Sun Princess.

'Sir Arnold Weinstock told me "If you want to get off ours and ride All Along, you can", but I decided to stick to my original plans. I had done the donkey work in the St Leger for Sun Princess; everything had gone right, and I got a share of the winning purse. I thought Sun Princess would probably win the Arc and I'd been promised a similar reward there. Who's to say I'd have won the Arc on All Along anyway?'

To be fair to Joe, and indeed to Lester, All Along had yet to hit the world class form which saw her enjoy a magnificent autumn. Winning the Arc was the start of it all. After that she improved and won the Rothmans International at Woodbine, the Turf Classic at Aqueduct and the Washington International at Laurel. On top of the huge winnings, an insurance policy had been taken out to guarantee any horse winning those three North American races a million-dollar bonus. Though it didn't bother him Joe admits that he reckoned up the percentage!

Joe had reason to be fairly optimistic at the beginning of the 1984 Flat season. He was now riding quite a number of horses for the young Upper Lambourn trainer Charlie Nelson, the son of Peter Nelson, who had trained Snow Knight to win the 1974 Derby. In 1983 Charlie had won the Middle Park Stakes with Creag-an-Sgor ridden by Steve Cauthen, a race in which Joe had again teamed up with Henry Cecil on the favourite and third

Mahogany becomes favourite for the 1,000 Guineas as a result of this fluent win at Newbury.

home Vacarme, owned by Daniel Wildenstein. Stable jockey Lester Piggott had at that stage announced that he wouldn't be riding All Along in the Arc and in fact was never to ride for Wildenstein again. Charlie Nelson, though, was reckoned to have an even better two-year-old in the filly Mahogany, owned like Creag-an-Sgor by the Tulloch family. 'She looked like being a very good filly at two. I didn't ride her first time out at Newbury but I'd ridden her at home and thought she was a certainty. I then won the Rockfel Stakes at Newmarket on her and she went into the winter strongly fancied for the Guineas.'

Mahogany's trial was the Gainsborough Stud Fred Darling Stakes and on the strength of a decisive win she was made 6–5 favourite for the 1,000 Guineas. But she could manage only sixth place behind Pebbles and went down with the virus shortly

afterwards. Joe doubts that she was right on the day and says that when she came back she never worked as well again. Joe and Charlie Nelson got the Newbury trial double-up when Creag-an-Sgor won a mediocre Clerical Medical Greenham Stakes, but he too was well beaten in the 2,000 Guineas.

That spring Joe and Henry Cecil had a successful reunion with the Wildenstein-owned Legend of France in the Earl of Sefton Stakes at Newmarket. Legend of France was a beautifully bred colt by Lyphard out of the Oaks winner Lupe. Lupe had already produced Leonardo da Vinci and L'Ile du Reve, which won the 1979 Cheshire Oaks for Henry and Joe. Joe had ridden the colt in the Petition Stakes at Newmarket at three when he had trotted up by 12 lengths. In the Earl of Sefton, Lester Piggott was on Henry Cecil's other runner Adonijah (9–2) but Joe beat him

Joe punches home Legend of France for Henry Cecil and Daniel Wildenstein in the Earl of Sefton Stakes. Stable jockey Lester Piggott was on the runner-up, Adonijah.

181

by a length and a half on the 4–1 favourite. It was nice to see Joe punching home a winner in the familiar Wildenstein colours of royal blue with light blue epaulets in which he had had so much success with Henry Cecil.

Legend of France then ran in the Prince of Wales' Stakes at Royal Ascot but ran badly and was undoubtedly suffering a recurrence of the lameness that had affected him before. After the race Joe remembers there was a big dust-up. 'Henry was called everything, not by the old man but by his son Alex Wildenstein.' It wasn't long after that that Henry Cecil lost the Wildenstein horses.

Time Charter was of course still in training. Joe was all set to ride her in the Coronation Cup: her regular rider Billy Newnes was out of the reckoning this time because of a Jockey Club ban after he was alleged to have accepted a bribe from a professional gambler. Newnes wasn't to ride again until the 1986 season. But then Joe himself fell foul of the stewards in France.

In the Prix Dollar at Longchamp on 27 May Joe had partnered Andre Fabre's Mourjane into second place behind his stable companion Mourtazam. There are two winning posts at Longchamp and Joe dropped his hands at the first of them when there was still a few more yards of the race to run. Mourjane looked held by his stable companion at the time anyway and the seven-day ban imposed by the French stewards looked harsh in the extreme. It meant that Joe missed the whole of Epsom and therefore the winning ride on Time Charter in the Coronation Cup. Steve Cauthen deputised but anybody could have done because Time Charter was brilliant. Before the race she had drifted, from 7–4 joint favourite with her great rival Sun Princess, out to 100–30, but there were no indications that she was in need of the run. She quickened past Sun Princess in the final furlong to win very easily by four lengths.

Joe was watching from the stands, assisting John Oaksey for Channel 4 Racing. Joe's tips were so accurate that he received umpteen letters of thanks, one of which said: 'Thanks to you, we have enough money to take our wives on holiday'. As viewers will know, Joe had a marvellous first season as a part-time presenter on Channel 4 in 1986, highlighted by Midway Lady's 10–1 win in the 1,000 Guineas. Joe had nominated her after seeing her in the paddock.

Joe was back on Time Charter in the Coral-Eclipse. He says: 'There were a lot of problems in the race and I didn't get a clear passage through. I got a break at the death on the inside but Pat Eddery on Sadlers Wells was coming across me from the outside

Joe was an instant success as a television tipster. He prepares with John Oaksey to go on air on Oaks day in 1984.

and tightening us all up. I therefore had to check and switch left. She picked up well but the chance had gone and we were beaten a neck. I wanted to object after the race.'

Many people thought that Time Charter had been an unlucky loser and she was made a short-priced favourite at 6–4 to follow up her 1983 win in the King George at Ascot and to become the first since Dahlia to win the race twice. Joe gave Time Charter a very similar ride to the previous year, holding her up for a late run, only this time Lester Piggott set a much faster pace on the front-running 1983 Derby winner Teenoso. 'Lester jumped out of the gate as though the devil was behind him and never let up the whole way. It was a great ride and broke Grundy's track record.'

Time Charter finished fourth just a head in front of Sun Princess. For Joe though she was never quite the same mare after the Eclipse. 'Henry Candy's stable had a virus throughout that season and really her fourth at Ascot wasn't a bad effort. I think Henry thought that she may have wanted some more cut in the ground as she was beginning to feel the old legs a bit by then.' Time Charter raced only once more, a disappointing run in the Arc. 'I wasn't asked to ride her there so I assume connections hadn't been pleased about the Ascot performance!'

In the autumn of 1984, it looked, after a long, lean spell, as though Peter Walwyn had a potentially top class colt on his hands in Khozaam, a son of Seattle Slew out of the brilliant Canadian mare Par Excellence.

Says Joe: 'Khozaam was a gorgeous looking horse and had a nice temperament. When he won first time out in the Granville

Khozaam bursts through to maintain his unbeaten record at Newbury.

Stakes at Ascot, Peter almost paid for his holiday out of it – he'd worked so well and Peter has a great record in that race. He then won his next two starts, on the second occasion, the Washington Singer Stakes at Newbury.' Joe had to ride at his strongest to win on that occasion. Khozaam didn't get a gap until very late on and then showed an admirable turn of speed to go through and win. He then ran a fine race when going down by a head to Paul Cole's Reach in the Royal Lodge Stakes at Ascot. 'I thought he would make a very good three year old but he never materialised.'

184

Khozaam was owned by Hamdan Al-Maktoum, one of three sons of the ruler of Dubai who have revolutionised British racing in the last decade or so. Joe's view is that they have been good news for the sport. 'They've created a lot of employment. Whatever they've done, they've done it well, particularly buying up and improving property. Money doesn't really concern them – they do it purely and simply for the sport of it all. Unfortunately, when I was at Henry Cecil's we didn't have any Sheikhs and for the most part I was only associated with Sheikh

185

Shmaireekh: 'a horse with a super action, beautifully balanced and athletic'.

Hamdan's horses at Peter's. It was a pity that we didn't have much of note. We need these sort of people in racing – how will we progress if they're not there? The big English owner/breeders seem to be in a minority nowadays.

'I haven't been involved socially with many of the Arabs, apart from Prince Khaled Abdulla who I think is charming. I haven't ridden many horses for him – Band and Raft are a couple that spring to mind. Aziz Bazam is a dear friend of mine from India and he is also a very close friend of Prince Khaled's. I remember once I spilled coffee on Prince Khaled's mac. 'Don't worry, Joe,' was all he said, "I'll send you the dry cleaning bill!" Fahd Salman is also a very nice person and it's typical of him that he goes out of his way to speak to me. He told me that he was disappointed I didn't train as he was going to send me half a dozen horses!'

Sheikh Hamdan had a good class handicapper at Peter Walwyn's in the big, black form of Shmaireekh. Joe describes him as 'a horse with a super action, beautifully balanced and athletic'. Shmaireekh won the valuable Craven Handicap at Epsom on Derby Day in 1985 which led to him carrying 10st 2lb in the Royal Hunt Cup with a 7lb penalty. 'In the event he ran a smashing race but was beaten by the draw when sixth to Come On The Blues'.

Another horse to do very well for Hamdan Al-Maktoum in 1985 was Luqman, who won five of his ten starts. He was one of four two-year-olds with which Peter Walwyn did particularly well in Joe's final season as a jockey, the others being Stalker (four wins), Nashia (three wins) and Sperry (two wins). Joe himself was also associated with another two-year-old trained by Charlie Nelson called Marouble, on which he won the Norfolk Stakes at Royal Ascot that year.

Says Joe: 'Stalker was very small, but perfect conformation-wise, and was an ideal two-year-old.' Stalker made all the running in both the Gimcrack and Middle Park Stakes to provide Peter Walwyn and Joe with their greatest success together of their five-year-partnership. In between Stalker, ridden by Joe, failed by threequarters of a length to give 4lb to Luqman (Nicky Howe) in the Mill Reef Stakes at Newbury to give Peter Walwyn a notable 1–2 in the race. As a result of those successes, Walwyn was among the leading dozen trainers for the first time since 1980. (Unfortunately, for various reasons, only Sperry trained on satisfactorily as a three-year-old and he won the Cork and Orrery Stakes at Royal Ascot.)

These wins in the highest class were a much needed tonic for the Walwyn–Mercer team, but nevertheless Joe had made up his mind to retire at the end of the 1985 Flat season. 'I told Pete about it in August of that year. We had a chat over a coffee and I said "I think I might retire this year – I just want to tell you now so that you've got time to fix up another jockey." I had promised Tony McGlone that I would manage him when I stopped racing.

'Towards the end, I was riding bad horses in races for which I should have been riding better ones. It's no fun when you go down and come back last time after time. Then you hear people muttering about you getting too old. When people start to talk like that, there's only one way out. Things like that hurt me and I thought to myself, if people don't think I can do the job, then I won't do it. I enjoyed my five years with Pete, he's a smashing guy to work for. It was just a pity that we didn't have some better horses.'

Retirement was also to mean more time for Joe to indulge in his favourite pastime – shooting. 'Harry Carr, my father-in-law, introduced me to shooting. I started off with a 20-bore and eventually began to shoot quite well. Gordon Richards was another keen shot and I bought his 12-bore guns from him many years ago and still use them. Doug and Eph Smith also used to come along, and I'll never forget Lester Piggott's first shoot. My father-in-law invited Lester to a shoot at Ousdon one winter's day. Lester and I were standing at the back waiting for the birds to fly over when a pheasant came running across the gateway. Lester took aim and blew it to smithereens! I ran across to pick up a mass of broken feathers and informed him: "You're not supposed to shoot it on the ground, Lester – you're supposed to shoot them when they're flying." It was the first bird he'd ever shot in his life!

'My old Guv'nors Jack Colling and Dick Hern used to give me the Monday off before the York Ebor meeting so that I could go shooting with Major Holliday. The Major used to invite jockeys to shoot grouse on that day. Mr Joel also held some fabulous shooting parties at Childwick Bury Stud. Dave Dick, Jimmy Lindley, Brian Taylor and myself would arrive late in the

'All right, Lester, you can put the gun down now!'

afternoon and the butler would take our baggage. We would have tea at five o'clock, and after a chat in the library the baths were prepared before we changed for dinner. The spread of food was tremendous. By this time the butler had laid out our clothes and belongings on the dressing-table. I remember Brian Taylor laughing aloud once when he returned to his room. All his things had been laid out, neat and tidy – including his old golf tees and his comb, which had about five teeth left in it. We stood there helpless with laughter. The social side of shooting is marvellous but it has become a very expensive sport. Fortunately I am invited to a lot of shoots.'

Joe's great rival, Lester Piggott, made a successful start to a training career in 1986 but Joe decided against training. 'We did think about it at one time, but I thought when I stopped riding I'd be comfortable enough to do what I wanted to do in the three or four months of the year I would have to myself. I didn't particularly want to work for the rest of my life. I still enjoy riding out at Peter Walwyn's, of course.'

Joe now acts as agent to both Brent Thomson and Tony McGlone. 'The pair of them had 996 mounts in the 1986 season. It was hard work getting the rides for them to begin with, but in the last three months of the season my job was made a lot easier because people began to 'phone me. I get a great deal of pleasure from hearing people saying that Brent or Tony have ridden well in a race.' The two young jockeys can only benefit from the advice of a man who has ridden Classic winners over four decades. 'I suggested to Brent that in a close finish it is always better to ride over the line than to it. To win by a short head, you have to ride not *to* the post but *past* it.' This was the sort of information that Joe passed on to the young apprentices in a lecture he gave at the Newmarket British Racing School last November. Joe had given similar talks over the winter of 1973–74 when he held clinics for Jamaican jockeys to demonstrate the skills and techniques of raceriding in an attempt to improve the standard of horseracing on the island.

Few would disagree that Joe Mercer was the most stylish rider of his era. He was also one of the strongest and yet used the whip sparingly. Under an article titled 'Merciful Mercer' which was published in November 1979, Peter O'Sullevan asked his *Daily Express* readers for their comments on the use of the whip. O'Sullevan wrote: 'Joe is singled out for his "sheer artistry and gentleness". A Northern man expresses the hope that in view of the results he has achieved without using the whip, other jockeys follow his example.'

Here are Joe's own comments: 'A lot of jockeys tend to go for the stick first. Some jockeys get more of a response from their horses by urging them with hands and heels and then using the whip when needed. A jockey riding at the top of his form will treat his rivals with contempt because he is oozing confidence. Pat Eddery, Greville Starkey, Walter Swinburn and Willie Carson are great examples. They will win a race by half a length when it could have been ten'. Joe adds that there was no particular jockey whom he found it difficult to beat in a finish. He explains: 'Over the years, riding against them every day of the week, you learn how much a jockey has up his sleeve as the climax of a race approaches. Lester used to sit as still as a mouse and would look as if he had a lot in hand, just squeezing it along. But if he went for it, he probably wouldn't find much. On the other hand, Willie would be pumping away on a horse three furlongs from home and you'd think he'd have nothing left. But his mounts find something – look at Petoski in the 1985 King George.'

Not all jockeys can use their whips in both hands. In Claude Duval's book *Pat on the Back* the author asked BBC commentator and race-reader John Hanmer for his comments on the top jockeys: 'The great thing about Pat Eddery is that he is completely ambidexterous ... Piggott is far better with his right hand but can use both ... Tony Murray, Joe Mercer and Geoff Lewis are like Eddery – ambidexterous. Joe Mercer is the best at using the stick in either hand. He has never rung up for a ride in his life and I think he is better than Piggott and Eddery but probably nobody will agree with me. To me, his win on Counsel at York in 1957 was the greatest display of riding I ever saw. Joe on Bustino in the Coronation Cup was poetry in motion. Also on Highclere beating Eddery on Polygamy in the 1,000 Guineas, and in defeat on Homeric by Mill Reef in the Coronation Cup. Age is no barrier in jockeyship' he continues, 'but I think Mercer has pulled more races out of the fire than any other jockey.'

One race in the 1985 season that was certainly won by brilliant handling on Joe's part was the Rowley Mile Nursery at Newmarket in October. He was on John Dunlop's Highland Chieftain who had won comfortably for Joe on his debut at Brighton in August. Entering the final furlong the race seemed to rest between George Duffield on Air Display and Brent Thomson on Auction Fever. But Highland Chieftain was responding to Joe's pushing, and with 50 yards to go, Joe went for a gap between the pair and got up to win by half a length. It just showed that, at 52, he was riding as well as he ever had and it was

190

a great pity that no more than a handful of trainers appeared to be aware of the fact.

But of course, Joe didn't have to work at his hardest for either of his two wins on his last day as a jockey at Doncaster on the final day of the 1985 Flat season. Joe's win on John Dunlop's Bold Rex in the big race, the William Hill November Handicap, his last ride, was the fairy-tale ending to a career that doesn't often happen outside old-fashioned novels. As Joe says, 'There was nothing wrong with what I did in my last year of riding and I finished on a great note. I'd got out on top of the tree.'

So how can Joe's 36-year riding career be summarised? Joe's friend and fellow ex-jockey, Jimmy Lindley, has the last word: 'Joe was the ultimate professional. As well as being the most stylish rider in the business and one of the strongest, he had horse sense. He knew how to make a young horse into a horse that was going to last. He had terrific balance, judge of pace – in fact everything that was needed, and perhaps a little bit more.'

Career Statistics

DOMESTIC RIDING RECORD 1950–85					
Year	Winners	Year	Winners	Year	Winners
1950	6	1962	85	1974	70
1951	15	1963	88	1975	93
1952	26	1964	106	1976	98
1953	61	1965	106	1977	102
1954	76	1966	88	1978	115
1955	77	1967	78	1979	164
1956	69	1968	68	1980	104
1957	73	1969	81	1981	64
1958	84	1970	78	1982	58
1959	87	1971	89	1983	55
1960	95	1972	91	1984	49
1961	87	1973	81	1985	43

Total: 2,810

DOMESTIC CLASSIC WINS

1,000 GUINEAS
1974 HIGHCLERE
1979 ONE IN A MILLION

2,000 GUINEAS
1971 BRIGADIER GERARD

OAKS
1953 AMBIGUITY

ST LEGER
1965 PROVOKE
1974 BUSTINO
1980 LIGHT CAVALRY
1981 CUT ABOVE

OTHER BRITISH GROUP ONE WINS

CORONATION CUP
1974 BUOY
1975 BUSTINO

ASCOT GOLD CUP
1967 PARBURY
1980 LE MOSS

KING'S STAND STAKES
1968 D'URBEVILLE
1969 SONG

ECLIPSE STAKES
1972 BRIGADIER GERARD
1978 GUNNER B

**KING GEORGE VI &
QUEEN ELIZABETH II
DIAMOND STAKES**
1972 BRIGADIER GERARD
1983 TIME CHARTER

SUSSEX STAKES
1971 BRIGADIER GERARD
1972 SALLUST
1979 KRIS

YORKSHIRE OAKS
1956 INDIAN TWILIGHT
1965 MABEL
1979 CONNAUGHT BRIDGE

CHEVELEY PARK STAKES
1964 NIGHT OFF

MIDDLE PARK STAKES
1964 SPANISH EXPRESS
1970 BRIGADIER GERARD
1985 STALKER

DEWHURST STAKES
1961 RIVER CHANTER

CHAMPION STAKES
1971 BRIGADIER GERARD
1972 BRIGADIER GERARD

In addition to his four St Leger wins, Joe Mercer has a fine overall record in the top class staying races:

HENRY II STAKES
1965 GREY OF FALLODEN
1971 CHARLTON
1975 ZAB
1976 SEA ANCHOR
1978 BUCKSKIN

GOODWOOD CUP
1979 LE MOSS
1980 LE MOSS

DONCASTER CUP
1953 NICK LA ROCCA
1964 GREY OF FALLODEN
1968 THE ACCUSER
1972 BISKRAH
1976 SEA ANCHOR
1978 BUCKSKIN
1979 LE MOSS
1980 LE MOSS

JOCKEY CLUB CUP
1953 AMBIGUITY
1969 HIGH LINE
1970 HIGH LINE
1971 HIGH LINE
1978 BUCKSKIN

PRINCIPAL OVERSEAS WINS

IRELAND
IRISH 2,000 GUINEAS
1973 SHARP EDGE
IRISH SWEEPS DERBY
1959 FIDALGO
IRISH ST LEGER
1965 CRAIGHOUSE

GERMANY
ARAL-POKAL
1975 LORD UDO

FRANCE
PRIX DE DIANE (French Oaks)
1974 HIGHCLERE
PRIX VERMEILLE
1970 HIGHEST HOPES
PRIX DU MOULIN
1972 SALLUST
PRIX ROBERT PAPIN
1971 SUN PRINCE

ITALY
PREMIO ROMA
1984 YAWA

MOST WINS BY RACECOURSE

NEWMARKET	226	KEMPTON PARK	96
BATH	205	GOODWOOD	94
NEWBURY	175	DONCASTER	88
ASCOT	148	LEICESTER	76
WOLVERHAMPTON	124	WARWICK	60
WINDSOR	123	YARMOUTH	58
SALISBURY	109	{ PONTEFRACT	54
BRIGHTON	104	{ BIRMINGHAM	54
NOTTINGHAM	102	CHESTER	48
LINGFIELD	101		
{ SANDOWN	100		
{ YORK	100		

Compiled by Dorothy Laird
Pacemaker, February 1986

JOE MERCER'S BEST HORSES –
BY TIMEFORM ANNUAL RATING

BRIGADIER GERARD	144
BUSTINO	136
{ KRIS	135
{ LE MOSS	135
SALLUST	134
BUCKSKIN	133
SONG	132
TIME CHARTER	131
{ CUT ABOVE	130
{ PROVOKE	130
{ ROYALTY	130
{ HIGHCLERE	129
{ HIGHEST HOPES	129

Index

BIBLIOGRAPHY

Queen's Jockey Harry Carr (Stanley Paul)
Eight Flat Racing Stables John Rickman (Heinemann)
My Greatest Training Triumph edited by John Hughes and Peter Watson
(Michael Joseph)
The Brigadier John Hislop (Secker & Warburg)
Race of the Century Christopher Hawkins (Allen & Unwin)
On The Level Henry Cecil (Harrap)
Pat on the Back: The Story of Pat Eddery Claude Duval (Stanley Paul)
Racehorses annuals (Timeform)